THE BUSINESS START UP GUIDE

ALAN PINK FCA CTA
ALISTAIR MACDONALD FCA CTA TEP

CONTENTS

Pink Proactive Publishing

The Business Startup Guide © 2021 Pink Proactive Publishing

For information contact:

Pink Proactive Publishing

44 The Pantiles, Tunbridge Wells TN2 5TN PPPublishing.co.uk

Book and cover design by Here Be Dragons Ltd ISBN: 978-1-9163566-2-7

First Edition: June 2021

10 9 8 7 6 5 4 3 2 1

CHAPTER 1
WELCOME TO A NEW LIFE

Welcome to PPPublishing's Business Start-Up Guide. We think you'll find this refreshingly different from some of the other advice you see in print and on the internet.

There's certainly no shortage of such advice, and you might wonder why we think a brand new book on this subject is needed. Well, apart from the fact that the world of business is constantly changing, and advice needs constant updating, we think we come at this from an unusual angle, and that this is likely to be useful in the real world to those looking to start up or build up a fledgling business.

For one thing we're not trying to sell anything. A lot of the advice you see, particularly online, is actually thinly veiled advertising for the services of whoever is giving it. All we're trying to sell is this book!

Secondly, our advice is anything but theoretical. It comes as a result of over 50 years combined experience of actually running a business, between the two authors.

Thirdly the aim of this book is to give you very practical, down to earth advice. So often what you get is a lot of waffle which makes it clear that the writer is simply looking around for things to say that sound good. Unlike some of those producing such material, we've learnt how to run business the hard way – by experience.

Finally, if it has no other merits, this book has what we would describe as the supreme merit of being short and to the point! You've got enough to do with your time, in the early stages of planning or running a business, without wading through some massive tome.

Should I or Shouldn't I?

A lot of people are very nervous about the idea of going self employed. It can feel like a bit of a leap of faith, stepping out into the unknown without the security of a regular pay cheque. But do bear in mind the (admittedly rather negative) point that a PAYE employment isn't, actually, so secure as all that these days. When our fathers and grandfathers (and, less frequently, mothers and grandmothers) signed on to work for an employer, they expected this employment to last for their whole lives, unless they decided to change for any reason. Those days are long past. In today's fast changing business world, employers (quite rightly) are very quick on their feet with redundancy notices, when the needs of the business so dictate. So, in setting up a paid employment as a secure option, contrasted with the chancy existence of the self employed, you may be guilty of some seriously out of date thinking. Even the public sector is not immune.

Another thing which may put people off taking the plunge in a new business is the red tape, rules and regulations that abound. It's true there is plenty of this, and more all the time: particularly if you can't avoid taking on employed staff (of which more later on in the book). But the demands of regulation are manageable: providing you know precisely what those demands are. This is one of the functions of this book. If you bear in mind that all of your business rivals are faced by the same requirements, you'll see that it's pretty much a level playing field in most cases.

And although we complain a lot about the rules and regulations in the UK, we get the strong impression that this is actually one of the easiest, least red tape ridden, jurisdictions in the world to do business. Many years ago now we were advising someone who was looking to set up a small business in Belgium. He told us that, under the rules there, before you entered into any business transactions at all you had to join the local Chamber of Commerce. This seems a reasonably un-onerous requirement: until you realise that the application process for joining the Chamber of Commerce was so complex that a separate profession had built up of guiding applicants through the nightmarish red tape of filling in the application form. He told us that it typically cost about €15,000 to get past this first hurdle; and, although that's a long time ago now and the rules may have changed, we think that this is by no means untypical of the burdens placed on businesses in other countries. We've also heard Italians complain bitterly about the bureaucracy there, and compare the UK favourably with Italy as a place to set up and do business.

Hobby or Business?

In the case of those lucky enough to be seriously interested in what they do, or propose to do, for a living (and don't worry if you're not one of these – these lucky people are a small minority) it can be quite difficult to put your finger on the exact moment when the hobby, which you do purely for enjoyment, becomes a business carried on for profit. This can be an important time to pinpoint, because it's then that you start needing to consider red tape requirements including, in particular, registering for tax. If in doubt, it's better to select an earlier date rather than a later, and then "officially" time the start of your business from that date.

Depending on the type of business, though, it can take a long time to move from officially starting to conduct your activities in a business like way, and the business actually showing a real profit. (We talk about a "real profit", because often businesses only seem profitable, in their earlier stages, because you, as the owner, aren't being paid for all the time you're putting in.) Don't let this slow march into profitability put you off.

That's the first very important lesson we hope people will learn from this book: things do take a lot longer to move into profitability than you expect. The thing is not to be "flaky" about this: business is a serious undertaking, earnestly pursued (to quote a judge in a case on whether business was being carried on) and you shouldn't give up if things don't go roaringly well right from day one. Perseverance is the key, and hardly anyone running a successful business today has had no setbacks or disappointments in the course of growing a business. Think of it as a delicate plant (at first) which needs constant attention and nurturing, but the fruit of which will well justify all the painstaking effort when it grows into a sturdy and robust tree.

Is all the effort worth it? Well, we can only say that there is nothing quite matching the satisfaction that you feel when the money starts coming in, and the business stops having to be constantly pushed, gaining a momentum of its own. If you are the sort that thinks this way, there's also a tremendous satisfaction in feeling that you are contributing to the local and national economy, and the general prosperity of the country.

Live on Millionaires' Row

Let's not be hypocritical, though. The reason most people carry on business is not for some supposed benefit to the community, but, to be blunt about it, to get rich. Take a walk along your local millionaires' row, or along leafy lanes, with large agreeable houses with swimming pools in the back garden, nestling amongst the trees. Very few of the owners of these houses work for someone else!

What this book isn't, to be clear, is one of those "self-help" manuals, which feed on people's dreams and try and make them think they can be another Carnegie, Richard Branson, or Sir Philip Green. These books proliferate, and the only people, we suspect, they really help to fame and fortune are the authors of the books themselves. Packed with punchy mottos, they make very good reading, and make you feel as though your horizons have been widened. That's how they manage to sell. But how many people actually derive any permanent benefit from reading "How to Become a Millionaire in Three Weeks", or other similarly titled works? Such books tend to make use of fine sounding mantras, like the often quoted motto "If you always do what you've always done, you will always have what you've got now". Quite from the fact that it doesn't take a genius to come up with statements such as this, it isn't even necessarily true.

So this book won't be letting you into any magic secrets about how to become immensely successful in business. That's because there aren't any. The boring fact of the matter is that it's hard work and persistence, and nothing else, that make the difference between a good idea that comes to nothing, on the one hand, and a profitable business on the other.

In the pages that follow you'll find out:

- How to plan the business in advance of starting it, and how to write a formal business plan if this is required for finance;
- What sources of business capital there are out there, and which are likely to be the most accessible to you in your business;
- How you should keep records, financial and otherwise;
- How to deal with the thorny question of taking on staff; or avoid taking on staff if this is possible;
- A summary of all the "red tape" requirements that you'll be up against;
- Amongst these, whether you need to register for VAT, and whether this could be an advantage even if it isn't a requirement;
- How to advertise and promote the business;
- How to choose and use accountants and other advisers, and what so called "experts" to steer clear of;
- How to structure the business tax efficiently (for example whether to use a limited company or not);
- What sort of overheads you are likely to incur, and how to control them;
- How to avoid the most common mistakes made in business;
- How to protect your business and personal assets from things going badly wrong;
- What the crucial difference is between working in the business and working on the business; and
- Where to find expert help when it's needed.

Hopefully this book is short enough to read in a single

sitting, if you want to. In that way you can get on with important business of doing rather than thinking about. But we hope, also, that it will be useful as a handbook to keep with you as the business progresses. Good luck, and here's to prosperity!

CHAPTER 2
THE BUSINESS PLAN

We've set our face, in this book, against the use of glib mottos which sound good but aren't actually much help in practice. So we won't begin by solemnly assuring our readers that "Failing to plan is planning to fail"; nevertheless, anything we do in life, from going for a walk to constructing a house, tends to work out better in the end if we start out by giving it a little thought. And, depending on what you're doing, in the business context you might say that the more thought and planning goes into it, the better.

Not all start-up's need a "full dress" business plan. You know the kind of thing we mean, a 100 page bound glossy document with photographs, pie charts, and professional artwork. In some cases the plan can be just in your head. But there does need to be a plan.

The question of how elaborate the business plan should be depends on the reason why you're preparing it. And there are basically two quite separate reasons for drafting one:

- To clarify your own thoughts on how the business should be developed, and act as a kind of check as the business progresses; and

- To present the business prospects in the best
  possible light for possible lenders or investors.

It naturally follows that the type of business plan you draw up will be different, depending on whether it's aimed just at you and those working with you in the business on the one hand, or at attracting outside interest on the other. You might even do two plans – or rather, two versions of the same plan, one for internal and one for external use, so to speak.

Should you draft the business plan yourself, or get someone else to do it? Most accountants will offer you help, or even draw up your plan for you, if you ask them; and there is a whole army of more obscurely qualified "business consultants" who will leap at the chance.

Our answer to this question is not so much that it's advisable for you to draw up the plan yourself, as that it's fundamentally impossible for anyone else, other than you as the creator of the business, to do so. The ideas and the thinking must be yours, otherwise it isn't your business, or your business plan. Ultimately the success of the business will depend on your care and attention given to it, along with that of others working in the business, and you and they need to "own" the thoughts and ideas set out in the plan.

But don't despair if you always got C minus for English composition at school, or even if your grasp of numbers is as shaky as that of the average politician. Whilst the fundamental outline and skeleton of the plan needs to come from you, there is plenty of outside help available, both before and after the basic planning process has been undertaken by you.

First of all, of course, there's this book you're reading! In this chapter, we give you a skeleton, or framework around which to build your planning – and this is relevant even if your plan is the sort which is simply in your own head. You can either use the titles we've suggested as chapter headings for a massive tome at one extreme, or you can use them as a quick "check list", to ensure that you've thought of all the important aspects, at the other extreme.

We're not claiming that our suggested format for a plan is the only correct one, and all others are "wrong". Just as no two businesses are the same, so no two business plans are: it may be that you need to add new sections, not mentioned below, in your own business context. But if you miss out any of the aspects we've listed, you need to ask yourself whether the plan might be seriously deficient in an important respect.

So let's have a look at the various sections of a "typical" business plan.

Introduction to the Business

This is a very important part of the document for external users. Most of these people will start by knowing absolutely nothing about the business idea, or what the jargon terms, with which you may be familiar, mean. So don't take any knowledge in the reader for granted but spell out in simple terms what the business idea consists in, the bits about the industry in which it operates that an outsider may not know but needs to be aware of, and where the proposed business will precisely fit into that industry.

Having spelled out the ABC, the next thing to try to do is to enthuse the reader about the business idea. As, at this stage, we are talking about a brief introduction, don't go into tremendous technical detail at this stage: but if you feel that your business idea is excitingly different from others, this is the time to major on that difference. What makes your business idea special? And not just what makes it special in general terms, but also what's special about it that makes it likely to succeed financially. This is part of the plan where you may well call in outside help, if the eloquent use of English isn't your strong point. But obviously you do need to convey your enthusiasm to the writer, if he or she is going to express it adequately in the introduction to the plan.

The Market

We think a description of the market for the business' goods and services should come very early on in the plan, because a business doesn't just exist for its own sake, of course, and no matter how wonderful the idea, and how efficiently its costs can be controlled, sales are the most essential ingredient in any business.

So think a lot about your market. Who will buy your product, what sort of person are they, how many of them are there, and why are they arguably inadequately served by other businesses currently operating in the same industry?

The answer to this last question might simply be that your product is markedly better than the other ones that are available!

There's almost no limit to the amount of detail and effort you **can** go into in your analysis of the market. The two extremes here are, on the one hand, an intuitive grasp of the fact that there are loads of potential buyers out there; and the other extreme, an expensively commissioned market research study, of the sort which supermarkets do before opening up a new line. How far you go in your market research depends on how much you have in the way of resources of time and money, and also whether the particular business idea you have demands it. In some cases, the existence of a substantial market for the goods or services of your business is obvious, and in those cases you need to concentrate on what marks you out from the competition (of which more later).

Promotion and Marketing

Because, at the end of the day (and indeed the beginning) sales are what business is about, the next most important part of your planning process, after deciding who your market is, is to work out how you are going to try to reach them. And here, from our own experience of starting up and running businesses, we have two very important messages, which you'll find more about in Chapter 8.

From the point of view of the business plan, what you need is a credible and practical method of putting your product or service in front of the public, and you'll need to set out what that is, and how much (if anything) this process of business promotion is likely to cost.

Competition

If you are very fortunate indeed, this section of the business plan may be very short! For most businesses, though, there will be a number of competitors all trying to make money out of the same market, and some of them are very formidable competition. The main point of this part of the business plan is to identify who they are, look at how much information we have about their scale and methods of operation, and above all, to consider whether there is anything we can learn about the way we should be running our business from the way they run theirs. If, for example, a major business rival, of a similar size and in a similar geographical market, completely fails to follow up what seem to you to be obvious lines of action, consider why this might be. What actually makes you different, if anything? This can be a salutary exercise to those who feel that they can walk straight into a booming market. Ask yourself what **really** makes you different? And put it all down in the plan.

The Required Investment

Again on the principle of putting the most important things first, we would suggest your next section should focus on how much money the business will need to get off the ground. A potential investor or lender to the business will be impressed by your down to earth approach, as no doubt many of them read a lot of very airy fairy plans which are light on the most basic, and most crucial detail, of which this is an example.

The actual number, in terms of how many pounds and pence is required, is obviously a function of your profit and loss and cashflow projections, which we will be coming on to next; and in the real world it is likely that the amount of investment required can't be predicted with any great accuracy. This is a fact of life which any sensible investor will be aware of, and the plan should include suggestions as to how you are going to deal with a requirement for more finance later on in the process, if it turns out to be needed. This might, for example, be bank overdraft finance or another call on investors.

Clearly this section of the plan needs to be fairly specific about what type of investment you are looking for, as well as how much. By the type of investment, we mean whether you are looking for a loan (and if so, whether this would be short term or long term) or equity investment. The next chapter of this book is about raising business finance, and may help clarify the thoughts of some readers on this very important question.

Profit and Loss and Cashflow Projections

The accountants in us are telling us that this is actually the most important part of the plan. The purpose of doing profit and loss and cashflow projections (the two are quite different from each other) is to see whether you have a business which is fundamentally likely to work financially or not. If not, then you need to scrap these ideas and come up with something else, if you really want to be in business. But possibly those who are more realistic about what businesses are actually like in the real world, as opposed to accountants' theory, would be inclined to take this view with a pinch of salt. P&L and cash projections depend on a huge number of assumptions, of course. And therefore the assumptions are extremely easy, in practice, to "tweak" to give very different results, some of which say that the business will make you a millionaire in six months, and some of which that it doesn't have a hope.

So probably, apart from a basic "sense check" (for example does your business require 100 million people in the UK to buy your product?) the purpose of these arithmetical models is just to show prospective investors that you have a potentially viable business idea.

In our typical business plan, the financial projections will come at the end as an appendix, rather than clogging up the main body of the report, which is otherwise in words; but there's no "right" or "wrong" place to put these. In the narrative part of the report, though, you should explain the projections in words, because an awful lot of people reading the business plan will glaze over when they see a spreadsheet with lots of figures on it. So you need to make it easy for them, and also set out the key assumptions on the basis of which you've shown that your business is a viable one. More about the process of drawing up financial projections just below.

Contingency Plans

The one thing you can be sure of, in starting a business, is that things won't go as planned. What marks out a good business plan from an indifferent one is that it makes it clear that this inevitable fact of life has been appreciated and allowed for in the planning. What if sales are X% less than anticipated? What if new capital expenditure is needed earlier than expected? What, precisely, is most likely to go wrong, and what will be the impact on the business if it does? If the plan can show that the business is sufficiently resilient to deal with contingencies, this will make it a lot more impressive to the reader.

CV's

Anyone wanting to invest in a business, particularly a new business, will want to know, if they are sensible, enough about the people running it to give them confidence. So you should set out reasonably detailed CV's of the main person, or each of the main people, obviously majoring on any aspects of their past experience that are relevant to the business and, perhaps implicitly rather than explicitly, explaining why they happen to be "at a loose end" and wanting to being involved in this new business. This is something which many investors tend to be understandably cynical about: is he starting out on his own because no-one else will employ him?.

The Appendices

As we say, often the financial projections are pushed to the back of the document, and the reason for this is to avoid interrupting the narrative flow of the plan. The main body of the plan should explain and summarise what conclusions are to be drawn from the financial projections, and give the assumptions on which they're based. But the actual figures need to stack up in themselves, for those who are able to read and understand spreadsheets. One aspect of the actual setting of assumptions and calculation of the numbers that shouldn't be underestimated is the amount of time a new business actually takes to get established. It's almost a golden rule that this is a lot longer than you think! So beware of over-optimistic assumptions about the growth of turnover, in particular, when you are doing the projections. The preparation of such spreadsheets is something you could sensibly delegate to somebody else if you are not particularly an Excel wizard. But it needs to be you that feeds the preparer (it might be your accountant) with the necessary basic input figures and assumptions.

Another aspect which is often relegated to the appendices to the business plan is specific technical information about the business. It may be necessary to include this to show those who are able to understand the technicalities that the business is based on a sound idea. Clearly you need to be careful about giving away, to third parties, essential information which perhaps gives you a head start over the competition. But this aspect of things can usually be dealt with by ensuring that the reader signs a suitable non-disclosure agreement.

The "Rolling" Business Plan

So that sets out the important aspects that we think any business worth its salt should cover. As we say, all businesses are different, and it's not necessary to put your thinking in any kind of "straitjacket". But hopefully, even if you don't copy the subject headings verbatim, this would give you at least a starting point for thinking about what matters.

Going forward, it's a good idea not simply to put the business plan in your bottom draw and forget about it, but to check the actual progress of the business against plan. Sometimes important actions that you would otherwise have forgotten can come to light as a result of this process: and where the actual experience of trying to start the business is markedly different from your assumptions when you were forming your plans, it can even be a good idea to revise or rewrite the business plan to take account of your actual experience to date. A careful comparison of projection to actual could even lead you to change radically the direction that you had started the business going in.

CHAPTER 3
RAISING BUSINESS FINANCE

To be frank, you're fortunate if the type of business you are looking to start up doesn't require a capital injection – they don't all. And generally speaking those who only need to raise a little money are a lot better off than those who need to raise a lot. But there undoubtedly are sources of finance for business start-up's out there, and the main ones are:

- Bank borrowing
- Your own funds
- Borrowing from friends or relations
- Crowdfunding
- Sale of Equity; and
- Funding from the public sector

We'll have a look at each of these in turn, because different sorts of finance are appropriate for different sorts of business start-up situations.

Bank Borrowing

Our apologies in advance if this section seems a bit cynical: but remember we are not trying to sell anything in this book. What you'll get here is a realistic view of the merits of borrowing from the bank, and your chances of your application for credit being approved.

But first, a word about bank finance brokers. These seem to proliferate, to judge from a cursory search of the internet, and their professed skill is to act as an intermediary between you and the bank, helping you to secure finance that you may not have been able to get without them; or on better terms. Like any other learned profession, business finance brokerage contains the good, the bad and the ugly practitioners. A book like this can't possibly help you find the good ones, because these change from week to week; but we can give you a pointer about the general merits or otherwise of engaging with these advisers.

The main advantage of a bank finance broker is that they know where not to bother asking. This may seem like a rather negative benefit, but it's possible that they may be able to save you from wasting a lot of time on fruitless loan applications. But we're not at all convinced that the converse, that of knowing where is good to look, is necessarily a skill that brokers major in. And this brings us on to what we've found to be one of the major disadvantages of brokers. This is their tendency to make sweeping statements about what can be achieved and what can't. We wish we had a fiver for every time a broker has assured one of our clients that lenders will not lend to a given proposition, or a proposition structured in a certain way, when we've got tangible evidence, in the situation of another client, that such borrowing is indeed possible. So if you do use a broker, take what he says with a pinch of salt when it comes to what **can't** be done. And the other disadvantage of brokers, of course, is that they cost you money. I don't say they don't necessarily earn that money on occasions, for example if they are more skilled than you at presenting the information in a sufficiently professional and "glossy" way to impress the banker. But sometimes you get the opposite feeling, (like, on occasions, with estate agents) that they earn their money easily.

Enough about brokers. Let's move on to the more interesting subject, arguably, of the types of bank finance that are available. If you watch television, and listen to commercial radio, read magazines, or go on the internet, you will get the impression that the "big name" banks are falling over each other to lend you money. But how does the actual reality match up? In the real world there are basically two sorts of bank loan available, and these are:

- Small unsecured loans; and
- Asset finance

Typically, at the time of writing, banks will lend you up to about £25,000, if they like your business proposition, without security. We should stress that if you had anything that the bank can secure lending on, like a property, the bank is likely to want to get its claws into this. But the harsh fact of the matter is that, if you haven't got any security, you can wave goodbye to any idea of borrowing large sums from the bank.

Although banks differ and it's well worth surfing the net to do your own research, typically banks will consider applications for loans of up to £25,000 on this small, unsecured basis. If you're going for one of these, we would suggest you read carefully Chapter 2 on how to write business plans, because you'd be missing a trick to approach the bank manager without one, especially given all the competition there is for the amount of money they have to hand out.

Some banks' websites will even give you a kind of automated algorithm, telling you how likely the computer thinks you are to gain approval; but again at the risk of seeming cynical, our own impression is that only a comparatively few such loan applications, and those for the most "gold plated" types business, are likely to succeed, and repay the very considerable amount of effort that needs to go into such an application.

Asset Finance

So now we move on to the other sort of bank finance, about which it is generally true to say that your application is much more likely to be successful, if your circumstances are right, than an application for an unsecured loan; and the only type of finance which is likely to amount to very much money at all. This is asset finance. If the money is needed for specific types of equipment, or vehicles, for which hire or lease purchase deals are available, you will no doubt go down that road. In the majority of cases, though, the asset referred to is going to be property: land and buildings. This might be the asset that you are looking to raise the finance to buy, for example a workshop or restaurant premises; or it may be an asset you own, even your own home, outside the business which has sufficient value and equity in it to form the basis for secured lending.

The best form of asset to re-finance to raise money for a business is buy to let property, if you've got it. Our experience is that raising finance on let properties like this involves less "red tape" (although these days, it still involves quite a bit of that) than borrowing secured on your own home. But home loans are possible: just don't rely on a bank lending you much more than 60% of its value.

"Second Tier" Banks

As we say, beware of brokers' sweeping statements. If you can't get a loan from one of the big banks, consider one of those newcomers, or second tier banks, that may be more willing to lend to you. Why? Because, very often, they are trying to break into the lending market, and are therefore less likely to be strangled by overstrict lending criteria. At the time of writing, Metro Bank is one of these "new kids on the block", as is Handelsbanken, the Swedish bank who have recently massively expanded their UK office network. We've found dealing with Handelsbanken like a breath of fresh air, because they are actually old fashioned in their approach. This may sound paradoxical, but some of us still in business are old enough to remember the time when bank managers were locally based, with local discretion on lending. Which meant that the person you were talking to knew all about your business and the area it operates in. Now, the big banks seem to have retreated completely from this (although some will deny this), and lending decisions are all made, it seems, by some remote committee or even computer. As we say, these are generalisations; and it's also true to say that the industry is changing fast. But it is much easier and pleasanter to deal with a bank like Handelsbanken where the personal, and local touch is so evident. (This book is not sponsored by Handelsbanken!) and to end our section on bank borrowing on a positive note: it's undoubtedly true to say that there is no golden rule, absolutely unbreakable, about what kind of application will work and what won't. Do shop around different banks and types of banks, and don't be put off by your first (or even second) refusal!

Your Own Finance

Using your own resources to fund your business is obviously the easiest form of finance there is, if you have the resources, as you don't have to convince a sceptical lender!

Not many people have large lumps of cash sitting around in the bank just waiting to be put into a new business start-up. But don't forget that there are other kinds of liquid assets, that you may be less generally aware of. For example, you might have an ISA which you've been quietly feeding with small amounts monthly for some years: has this grown to a substantial enough amount of money, sufficient to get you started? Or similarly, you might have an endowment life insurance policy of the type which can be cashed in.

And then there are pensions. These must rank highest of all on the list of forgettable assets – largely because they aren't "assets" in the same sense as cash, shares, ISA's, and life insurance bonds. What we mean is that pensions are essentially trusts where money is held for your benefit, but is not under your immediate control.

But it is sometimes possible to access pension monies to finance a new business, and there are a couple of ways of doing this.

Pete is a freelance DJ who has squirreled away a decent proportion of his earnings over the years into a personal pension. Now, at age 55, he wants to hang up whatever it is that DJ's hang up when they retire, and start his own record label. To do this properly needs a cash injection of £100,000, he reckons, and it just so happens that his personal pension fund is worth four times that. So, with all due taking of IFA advice etc etc, he elects to take the 25% tax free lump sum out of his personal pension, which provides him with the £100,000 injection of capital the new business needs.

The "catch" with this idea, for those under 55, is that you generally need to have reached this age before you take any of the benefits out of your pension. Personal pensions aren't allowed to lend money to your business, either. On the other hand, if you have reached the magic retirement age under your pension scheme rules, you aren't, of course, limited to the 25% tax free lump sum. Nowadays you can take the up to the whole amount out of your pension, albeit at a cost of paying income tax on the portion over 25%.

More ambitious planning using your pension fund monies, which is probably appropriate where larger sums are required (because of the costs involved) is illustrated in our second example.

Georgina is a high flying executive who has had some reasonably chunky pension contributions made into an occupational scheme for her by her employer. In a change of direction, she decides to throw up her glittering career in the city and start a "cottage industry" making fair trade knitwear. Being a dynamic and persuasive type, she already has firm commitments from a number of department stores: so now she just needs the premises and the machinery. Having consulted a specialist pensions administrator that does pensions which are given the abbreviation SSAS (Small Self Administered Scheme) she transfers her occupational pension rights from the employer's scheme to a new SSAS set up for her newly formed company. This enters into a loan agreement with the company, under which the funds are lent to it on a five year loan at a commercial interest rate.

. . .

As always where you are "messing around" with pensions, you need to make sure you have specialist advice before exploring avenues of the type set out in the examples above: but you could be pleasantly surprised to find that you have the funds available all wrapped up in your pension scheme!

Friends and Relations

We suspect that a high proportion of new businesses are actually funded by friends and relations of the embryo entrepreneur. But this sort of finance has to come, we think, with a very big health warning. There's nothing that can ruin a friendship, or a family relationship, more effectively than borrowing money which gets lost in a failed business. Think two or three times before going down this road, and, we would suggest, only go along it if there is no other feasible source for the cash.

There are basically two ways that you can structure finance from friends and relations. You can either give them an equity share in the business, or you can set up the amount as a loan, no doubt with proper interest payable on it.

A loan is a reasonably easy thing to arrange, and agree the key features: which are rates of interest and terms of capital repayment. Generally speaking, we understand that, if there's no agreement as to when the loan should be repaid, it can technically and legally be demanded back at any time. So, even if it's only in an informal communication like an email, do set out these essential terms of agreement to avoid potentially distressing misunderstandings later on.

If you give your friend or relation equity in the business, this brings into play questions of how the business should be structured. There are three main types of business structure to consider, which are partnership, limited company, and limited liability partnership or LLP. The choice of business structure is very important from a number of angles, particularly the tax angle, and we'll deal with that elsewhere in this book. Suffice it to say, here, that a partnership or LLP structure tends to be a lot less formal in the way equity is introduced and withdrawn than a limited company. Where you have a limited company to run your business, the equity injection will take the form of subscription for shares in the company, which give their own fixed rights over the governance and income of the company. Think carefully about these, as if you or your investor have any particular stipulations you can always give different shares special rights.

Crowdfunding

This is certainly the new kid on the block as far as business funding is concerned. At first sight, you might think that crowdfunding is an exciting new way to tap into investment from "ordinary" people such as yourself, with no real upper limit as to how much you could raise if your proposition goes "viral". For those who haven't really come across crowdfunding before, basically what it is is an internet based appeal for funds to those who find you the net, and are willing to chance their hard earned cash on your proposition.

As so often, though, the reality turns out to be less exciting than you would have thought at first glance. There are two sorts of crowdfunding, of which one is regulated by the Financial Conduct Authority and one isn't. The latter sort is the "reward" or "donation" based type of crowdfunding, which tends to be money raised for a good cause rather than simply to allow the person raising it to make filthy lucre from running a profitable business. You are allowed to reward investors in certain ways, but this sort of crowdfunding is quite distinct from the other sort, which comprises a commercial investment by someone intending to make a profit from it. This sort, the FCA regulated sort, is almost inevitably going to be done through an established crowdfunding platform that someone else has already set up. You'll find dozens of them by surfing the internet. So like any formalised arrangement involving heavily paid professionals, this type of finance raising can be time consuming and expensive, and is by no means a magic money tree. We suspect that the businesses most likely to succeed in raising money through crowdfunding are the "interesting" sorts of businesses, involving entertainment, celebrities, or popular activities. Plastic extrusion moulders probably need not apply! In short, it's quite a specialist area, and this is perhaps shown by the fact that crowdfunding has by no means elbowed out of place the other sources of business finance that we're talking about in this chapter.

Sale of Equity

Unless you are talking about the sale of shares in your company, or a share in your partnership or LLP, to friends and relations, as per the discussion above, offering the shares of your business for subscription is only for the very big boys, because not only do you have to be a Public Limited Company (generally with a requirement to issue substantial share capital) but you are also bound by a lot of very expensive red tape in making what is known as a IPO (Initial Public Offering). We suspect that people in this league won't be reading this book!

Grants etc from Public Funds

A book like this, aimed at readers in the whole of the United Kingdom, can't possibly do justice to the plethora of local grant initiatives. These are always very locally based, and are generally aimed at encouraging the start up of businesses in underdeveloped areas. So we'll move on swiftly to the other type of public money that is available, in the form of government start-up loans. These can be loans of between £500 and £25,000 (at the time of writing) to start or grow your business. This is an unsecured personal loan, offered to UK residents who are 18 or over who have or plan to start a UK based business that's been fully trading for less than 24 months. At the time of writing the interest rate on these loans is 6% per annum, which is quite high in comparison with secured loans, but looks fairly favourable amongst the general competition of bank unsecured loans. The loan has to be repaid over a period of between one and five years, but the business start-up loan from government funds is by no means a fait accompli. A business plan has to be drawn up and, being the government, a bureaucratic application process needs to be gone through, and you are by no means sure of success. However, this has got to be a possibility for those who don't fit into the fairly narrow bank criteria for similar sorts of unsecured loans. Enough of this subject for now, because it's all on the website at www.gov.uk/apply-start-up-loan.

CHAPTER 4
HOW TO KEEP RECORDS

Any discussion of business record keeping these days has to take into account HMRC's "Making Tax Digital" programme. Their introduction to Making Tax Digital (MTD) reads:

"Making Tax Digital is a key part of the government's plans to make it easier for individuals and businesses to get their tax right and keep on top of their affairs... Making Tax Digital is making fundamental changes to the way the tax system works – transforming tax administration so that it is:

- More effective
- More efficient
- Easier for taxpayers to get their tax right."

How kind of HMRC and the government! In a selfless move aimed at making things easier for those of us in business, they are introducing this go ahead and beneficent programme. Funny that it has to be made compulsory, by passing laws and imposing penalties for those who insist on doing things the old "difficult" way! The reality of the situation is that MTD is a tool for HMRC to keep closer control over recalcitrant taxpayers. Notwithstanding the nauseating "spin" surrounding the introduction of the MTD programme, everyone has got to be aware of what this new regulatory burden on business requires from them, and so we'll start off this chapter by giving you the lowdown on what MTD is and how it works.

What Does MTD Mean for Me?

At the time of writing, MTD is only compulsory for VAT registered businesses with a turnover of more than £85,000. So if you're turning over less than £85,000 of taxable sales (of which more below), then you don't need to do MTD even if you are registered for VAT on a voluntary basis. We'll be talking more about VAT registration in a later chapter, but suffice it to say that these voluntarily registered businesses will also be brought into the MTD net, according to the information at the time of writing, for their first VAT return starting on or after 1 April 2022.

So are businesses which are below the VAT threshold, possibly because their income is exempt (for example buy to let landlords) in the clear? They are for a while, but any self employed business (that is partnerships or sole traders, and landlords with annual gross income over £10,000) will need to follow the rules for MTD for income tax purposes, starting from their next accounting period after 5 April 2023. So the writing is definitely on the wall for manual records, for all but the smallest of businesses.

What should those starting up in business now do about MTD? As a business start-up, you won't yet have much or any turnover of course, and therefore the rules won't immediately apply to you. But if it's almost certain that your turnover will exceed the £10,000 threshold, there's little to be gained, probably, from putting off the evil moment when you need to buckle under the MTD rules.

But what does this buckling under precisely consist in? Put simply, it means that you need to acquire and use a computer software program, for keeping your records, which is approved for MTD purposes. You can still keep records on a computer spreadsheet initially if you want; but if you do this, rather than putting the information straight onto the MTD software, you'll need to acquire "bridging software" to take the information from your spreadsheet to the MTD interface.

So, is our assessment of MTD as yet another regulatory burden on business a fair one? We think so, because firstly it involves new businesses in the not insignificant expense of buying software, and perhaps the even greater expense involved in becoming expert in the use of it, or employing someone else to do so; but also it is a potential distraction from the hundred and one really important things that you have to think about when getting a new business off the ground. So, however, the bureaucrats and politicians, who know little or nothing about business, have decreed it should be.

All of the above is dealing with the MTD requirements that apply to unincorporated businesses: that is businesses which are not run through limited companies. Perhaps surprisingly, MTD isn't yet mandatory for limited companies, or even subject to a planned mandatory start date, as yet. In practice, though, companies already have a requirement to submit their corporation tax returns online. So in one sense, they are much more advanced digitally than unincorporated businesses, and in another sense much less. At present it is still perfectly feasible, and may even be sensible, to keep manual records for a small company, and simply use an accountant's software to put the return in to HMRC at the end of the year. We are talking, after all, about business start-up's here rather than businesses which have grown to a significant size. However, if you are a digital fan, you will no doubt want to put your records on computer even if you do operate through a limited company.

How to Deal with All those Bits of Paper

You might think, if we're all going digital, that bits of paper will be a thing of the past. Those of us who have introduced, or tried to introduce, "paperless offices" will know the general falsity of this hope. And in fact there's quite a lot to be said for bits of paper, as we'll come on to explain. Whether you welcome or disdain all those little scraps of expense dockets, invoices etc, the key point, above all points, is to make sure that you have a complete collection of these. HMRC, if they look into your books and records, will quite likely want proof of all the expenses and outlays that are susceptible of such proof, and even if you scan these bits of paper in, there's a lot to be said for keeping the hard copy as well, in our view. So don't throw the bits of paper away, but keep them on some system whereby you can lay your hands on them again in the future without endless searching.

And here it's probably time to issue an awful warning. We think that, in the general enthusiasm for all things digital, which the MTD program is a symptom of, short term thinking has almost completely displaced long term thinking. But consider how quickly computer technology changes, and with it the media through which past information is kept.

Who has a floppy disk player nowadays? Of course, it's possible, at great expense, and delay as well, to find somebody who will translate your old media into new storage systems. But wouldn't it be much easier if you simply had the records in hard form stored away somewhere reasonably accessible to your office?

Again and again, too, we've seen the situation of serious "crashes" in computer systems wiping out essential information that can never be recovered. It may be great fun keying in everything on your keyboard, and watching the computer calculating everything instantaneously: but if you need to look back on your records in years to come (and you may well need to) can you be sure, if you have **nothing** except those computer records, that they will be readable at that potentially far distant time?

A similar issue arises with online banking. How quick, easy and convenient it is to log into your account online at any time of day or night, check your transactions and balance, and make payments! But if the Revenue ask for six year's bank statements as part of an in-depth investigation, are you going to be able to supply these?

The solution to these potential disasters and difficulties is what we can only refer to as "the paperful office".

Take suppliers' invoices as an example. The purpose for keeping supplier invoice records is twofold: firstly so that you can check the items, both at the time of receipt and later on; and second to act as an audit trail for your accountants or HMRC, who want to look into the nature of the expense at some subsequent time. So it might be perfectly sensible to keep the records of these invoices in two different ways, for the two different purposes. A scanned version of the piece of paper (or a saved version if it arrived digitally) could be referenced to the relevant payment made against that invoice (assuming you don't go in for a full "purchase ledger" system – ask your accountant about this). But hard copy, taken out of the envelope or printed out of the email attachment, could be kept in perhaps alphabetical order of supplier for easy reference for practical purposes. So, in this suggestion, the electronic version would be the audit trail and the hard copy version would be the practical checking medium.

Bank statements too, should, we would suggest, be printed out if you do online banking and don't otherwise receive statements. The printout could be an essential lifesaver if the bank are unable or unwilling to give you copies going far enough back to satisfy HMRC. And we'll be coming on to the tax record keeping requirements later on. For some, no doubt, all of this talk of the paperful office, and printing everything out, will seem hopelessly luddite. But, as we say, the proof of the long term pudding is in the eating.

Pre-Trading Period

In most cases where a new business is set up by an individual, there will be expenses incurred before everything is properly set up, including the business bank account and the accounting system. For example, an individual may well find it easiest to use his own credit or debit card to subscribe for or buy things on the internet, in advance of having a proper business bank account and business banking arrangements in place. Keeping track of all these expenses paid privately is obviously very important, as otherwise you will end up paying tax on profit you haven't made. Even so crude a system as copying your personal bank statements, highlighting the business items, and getting some kind of invoice printed out or saved (or preferably both) to match against that highlighted item would be a lot better than risking the item being overlooked. A summary of these, in the form of a kind of "expense claim" can then be submitted to the business once its bank account has been set up, and reimbursement duly claimed. Note that, subject to certain time limits, the VAT can be reclaimed on these pre-trading expenses if you then go on to register (see the VAT Chapter for more on this).

Don't Overlook the Big Things!

And then there's the elephant in the room: the capital items, or fixed assets, that aren't acquired after the business has commenced (which would be picked up in the accounting records of the business accordingly) but are brought into use by the business when it begins. The fact that these might have been owned by the entrepreneur and used entirely for private purposes before the business began doesn't mean that they shouldn't be recognised in the books, and proper tax relief claimed, when they start being used in the business as well. Obvious items are vehicles, such as your car, that are sometimes used for journeys relating to the business; and home computer equipment which is also so pressed into service. But this area often richly repays a bit of lateral thinking as well. What about the heating system, including the boiler, in the building which is used for business purposes? The tax rules relating to these can be fairly complex, but the chances are that your tax will be being dealt with by an accountant: who needs to know what equipment etc you have in use wholly or partly for the business, so that he can make the right decisions on what to claim. If in doubt put it down on a list of equipment brought into the business at its commencement, and let the accountant decide.

How Long Do I Have to Keep Records?

Here, there's a strict legal answer and a different practical answer. The strict legal answer for businesses in general is that records need to be kept six years, or in the case of unincorporated businesses, approximately six years, to 31 January after the end of the accounting period. If you fail to do this, HMRC can levy some pretty swingeing penalties, and these can apply for each year that the records haven't been kept – an awful warning for those who rely entirely on possible fallible digital records. But our advice to any business person, or indeed any individual who does tax returns, is to keep records for a lot longer than that, in fact. Our advice is that you should keep all records for at least 20 years. Our reason for giving this advice is in relation to the disaster scenario of HMRC enquiring and deciding (on whatever strength of evidence or otherwise) that you have been deliberately understating your tax. They have a legal right, where they can prove this, to go back and assess tax on you for up to a 20 year period. So it's obviously a very good idea to have the records going back that far in order to refute the Revenue's claims, if possible. Anyone who keeps their records just for the statutory minimum period risks escaping penalties for failure to keep records on the one hand, but succumbing to a very much greater effective "penalty" in the form of tax on extra "profits" that he can't prove he hasn't made.

Where to Get Further Advice

A lot of people are very worried about the record keeping requirements which the powers that be (principally the taxman) impose on everyone running a business, and this chapter, especially the part relating to MTD, may not have made those worries any less. If you're not naturally a tidy record keeper, use someone who is. Preferably, particularly in the cash-strapped early days of a business, you might find someone close to you, even in your own household, who can take over this side of things, whilst you are concentrating on the much more important aspects of developing the business. We say that this is "much more important" because, whilst efficient administration is very important, indeed essential, without somebody driving the business forward there would be nothing for them to administer. But having said that, businesses can and do fail for chaotic administration. If you've no one like that who can help you, and you really don't feel up to record keeping requirements yourself, you've really no option but to bring in professional help.

And our advice here is to make the perhaps counterintuitive point that the cheaper that advice is, the more practically useful it's likely to be. This is because of the way professional bookkeeping and accounting firms tend to be set up. In the most junior (that is worst paid) category you have the book-keepers, whose job is simply to get the raw data about financial transactions into the system. Above this you have junior accountants, senior accountants and partners. The junior accountants, who will deal with putting the bookkeeper's work into the form of balanced profit and loss accounts and balance sheets, will have a lot of practical knowledge about record keeping systems, although perhaps not so much as bookkeepers who are actually using those systems "at the coalface" from day to day. The senior accountants, at manager level within the accountancy firm, will spend most of their days reviewing the junior accountant's work and they are at one stage removed, as well as their time being more expensive. And then, at the top of the tree, you have the partner, who may have had no dealings with actual accounting records for many years, because he has risen far "above" that. A qualified accountant's time will be **really** expensive, and also probably well out of date as far as record keeping is concerned: because most partners, when they were juniors, will have been dealing with the accounting systems of 20 or 30 years ago.

CHAPTER 5
TAKING ON STAFF

Our apologies in advance for repeating a story which you will also find in Alan Pink's Practical Tax Planning for Business. But it's such a good story that it deserves airing here, we think: and above all, calling it a "story" isn't quite fair, because it's absolutely true.

A managing director, foreman and apprentice are standing outside a building which their company is working on. High up on the wall there is damaged light fitting, which is half hanging off the wall. As chance would have it, a ladder, long enough to reach up to that light fitting, is lying on the ground nearby. To any reasonable person, it's obvious what needs to be done, and the apprentice makes the suggestion: "I can nip up that ladder in no time and get the fitting screwed back into the wall properly." The MD, who has had many years of experience of employing staff, begs to differ.

"No, you wait here, don't go up the ladder, and wait for the foreman and me to come back with a tower scaffold, which we've got just round the corner."

What follows has all the inevitability of Greek tragedy. The apprentice ignores these instructions, sets the ladder up against the wall, and climbs up to the light fitting. Sure enough, as the fates will have it, he falls off the ladder and injures himself. As sure as night follows day, and aided by an ambulance chasing "no win no fee" lawyer, he sues his employer for compensation, regardless of the fact that he only injured himself by directly disobeying instructions. Those who've heard this sort of story before won't be at all surprised to hear that the tribunal decided in favour of the apprentice, and awarded compensation. What makes this story particularly piquant, though, is the principal argument brought by the apprentice in favour of his claim.

"What you failed to take into account is the fact that I am stupid. If you'd considered properly just how stupid I am, you wouldn't have left me alone. It's your fault." (Or perhaps it was his well-paid representative which made this point on his behalf.) A better example of today's compensation culture would be harder to find: and all absolutely true.

The important point to make though, once we've finished laughing at that story, is that anyone taking on staff is taking on a host of potential problems, caused by the ridiculously biased legal system, for whom the employer seems to be almost automatically in the wrong in any dispute with the employee.

It's not hard to guess how this situation has come about, in a democracy where employers have few votes, and employees many. And the attitude seen in microcosm in that tribunal hearing is reflected throughout the statute law of the United Kingdom.

Probably the biggest problem for an employer, and the biggest disincentive to take on staff, is the difficulty of getting rid of a staff member if their work is inadequate. Even if you go through all the process of verbal and written warnings set out in the employment law, you are still at the mercy of anyone who decides to claim "unfair dismissal". Except for truly extreme behaviour, which most bad employees aren't stupid enough to indulge in, you are never safe against a claim for unfair dismissal on ground of poor work, no matter how inadequate that employee is. As we're talking confidentially here, as it were, from employer to employer or potential employer, we don't mind expressing the view that, in an awful lot of situations, this problem of wanting to get rid of somebody, and not being able to, is solved by the magic word "redundancy". Making a person redundant is about the only comparatively safe way of dismissing that person, and what it effectively means is that you have to show, if put on proof, that the role that employee fulfils is no longer required because of changes in the business. We are not, of course, advocating anyone using deceitful practices like this, but the whole topic of employer David versus the Goliath of employment law leaves a nasty taste in the mouth.

And the difficulty of enforcing adequate service from an employee is only one of a long list of burdens that an employer takes on. There are strict rules about working conditions, health and safety, etc which are enforced against the employer by law, and then there is the obligation to look after the employee's tax liabilities for him/her (the PAYE system) and also make provision for his pension arrangements (the workplace pension system). More of these later.

Employee Rights

But where is all this tirade against the unfairness of employment law leading, you may ask? What place has it got in a book aimed at business start-up's? Well, our main purpose in ramming the problems of being an employer down the would be entrepreneur's throat, so to speak, is to urge businesses to consider alternatives to taking on people in direct employment. In most sorts of business, if things go according to plan, the time comes when the work is much too much for one person, or one person and their spouse/live in partner. But don't, we would counsel, just unthinkingly slip into the role of employer by taking someone on if there are other ways that you could get the same service at a reasonable cost.

We're thinking here about a number of other options: the genuinely freelance worker, the staff agency, and the third party company whose business is providing the kind of services you're after. What you might call the "headline" cost of using these third party services may be higher. But bear in mind that, with an employee, you got other costs which need to be factored in order to make a fair comparison. These costs include:

- Employer's National Insurance, currently at 13.8%, which has to be paid on top of the employee's gross salary;
- The cost of administering the payroll, workplace pension etc obligations placed on you as employer. Don't regard this as a zero cost item if you are doing all of this yourself: your own time has a value, and you could, perhaps, have been out there making profits for the business while you were, instead, poring over tax and NI deduction tables and HMRC guidance;
- The cost of fitting the workplace to meet all of what used to be known as the "Factories Acts" requirements, that having an employee at your premises imposes; and
- The requirement to pay compensation, and pay lawyers to argue for you, in the event of a dispute with an employee.

Not all of these costs completely vanish if you use third party or freelance workers, but a lot of them do.

Zero hours Contracts

In an effort to gain an unfair advantage over employees, or just to put themselves in a position where they can run a viable business (depending on your point of view) some inventive employers have developed the concept of the "zero hours contract". Whilst frowned on by the political left wing, these are still, currently, valid in law, and can be very useful where your actual requirements for someone's work don't fit into a neat and consistent "nine to five" routine.

Under a zero hours contract, you as the employer, don't have to give the employee any minimum working hours. By the same token, the employee isn't obliged to take work when you offer it. So far, that's looking like a feature of a "free-lance" or "self employed" relationship. But unlike a freelance relationship, you have the obligation to pay the minimum wage for the hours worked, to provide paid holiday, pay staff for work related travel, and pay them for being on call if that is one of the requirements of the job. You also have to provide rest breaks etc if you provide these to other employees who aren't on zero hours contracts. You can't forbid the employee to work for someone else, or sack them if they do, even if these stipulations are written into the contract and freely agreed to by the employee.

Self Employed Workers

Given that a zero hours contract isn't quite as good as a "pure" self employment relationship, you might ask, why not just take people on as self employed instead? The problem here is that, no matter what you, or the worker, call the relationship, lawyers can decide that it is one of employment if it meets certain criteria. These include the situation, for example, where the worker is seen as "part and parcel" of your business; is not allowed to send a substitute to work instead of himself; is paid on an hourly rather than piecework basis; and many other such criteria. So, where the position in law is unclear (and it often is) you might be better off just accepting the "employment" label for the relationship, and retaining, if you need it, the flexibility that the zero hours contract gives you.

Pay As You Earn

If you do accept that someone who works for you is an employee, or even if you're not sure, you will have to knuckle under to the PAYE system. This clever arrangement which makes employers responsible for their employee's tax has been around since just after the Second World War and works (from the point of view of the government and the employee) very well. HMRC issue a PAYE code to the employer, which is basically an instruction to allow a certain deduction before applying the tax rates and deducting the resultant tax figure from the employer's gross pay to give net pay. In addition, there are national insurance deductions based normally on the same gross pay figure, and a so called "employer's national insurance" impost on top of the gross salary (which is really neither more nor less than a "payroll tax" – another reason to prefer taking on people who are self employed).

The basic concept of PAYE is, thus, quite simple. But even simple systems can be time consuming and irksome, particularly if you're not the sort of person that feels at home with figures. In one sense the amount of effort involved in operating a PAYE scheme for a single employee is not much less than the amount of effort involved in administering a payroll of a 100 employees, and so for a small business the effort required to operate PAYE can be disproportionate.

Payroll bureaus were made for this sort of situation. We have found payroll bureaus, who basically take the raw data from you in the form of hours worked and pay due and convert this into a properly PAYE-compliant payslip and set of records, are very good value for money, and take one headache away from you that you don't particularly need, when you are trying to build up a fledgling business.

So when you are considering what a proposed new employee is going to cost you, factor in the cost of paying the payroll bureau, and leave all the worrying to them. They will also advise you, if they are doing their job properly, on complying with your workplace pension and similar requirements. Because they will obviously be keeping up to date with the changes in favour of the staff that the government likes frequently to put in place to curry votes, there should be no fear of you inadvertently failing to meet these ever changing obligations.

CHAPTER 6
THE RED TAPE

This isn't so much a chapter, more a checklist. One of the big problems which face business in this country (although arguably less than in many other countries, as we commented in the introduction) is the amount of government imposed red tape which every business is legally obliged to cope with. Handling red tape can be both time consuming and expensive; but we think the main issue, which probably puts a lot of people off starting in business at all, is not knowing what the requirements are, or where to look. So the following checklist gives the main areas, and gives some pointers to where to find more help (including, in some instances, elsewhere in this book):

1. VAT

VAT probably causes more hassle and anxiety for business than any other piece of red tape, and for this reason we've devoted a whole chapter to it: Chapter 7.

2. Payroll Etc.

Have a look at Chapter 5, on "taking on staff" for a description of your obligations here. In that chapter, we have recommended the use of payroll bureaus to take the headache away as far as you, the hard pressed business owner, are concerned. Payroll bureaux should also advise you on your obligations with regard to workplace pensions.

3. Employment Law

Employment law normally only becomes an issue when you have some specific problem with a staff member. The most common problem, of course, is wanting to get rid of someone! In this situation, don't do anything drastic or hasty, but speak to an HR Specialist (Human Resources). If you can, as we commented in Chapter 5, avoid taking on somebody as an employee (rather than a freelance service provider) at all.

4. Record Keeping and Accounts

You'll find what we hope is some very useful advice on record keeping in Chapter 4 of this book. It is a legal obligation, as we comment in that Chapter; as is the obligation to notify HMRC that you are running a business and are therefore chargeable to tax on the profits. Most (but not all) businesses will appoint an accountant at a relatively early stage in order to make sure that they keep clean with regard to the direct taxation red tape. You could try ringing the HMRC Helpline – if you enjoy being on hold for long periods and then getting not particularly helpful advice at the end of that period!

, House

generic name "Companies House" to all that red tap￼ ￼ comes about from operating as a limited company or LLP. Summed up, the obligations are to submit accounts each year (which can be in a highly abbreviated form set out in company law), do a "confirmation statement" which gives certain information about the control of the company or LLP, and notifying Companies House of changes in directors and other officers. Normally speaking, if a business appoints an accountant, the accountant sees to all of these Companies House requirements for the company or LLP.

6. Health and Safety

This is a notorious area of red tape, affecting not just businesses but anybody who owns any kind of premises except for the private home. Whilst there are professionals who specialise in health and safety issues, for most business start-up's it is going to be just a matter of common sense, aided by what you can find out on the internet.

7. Data Protection

The data protection regulations are by no means straightforward, and have changed since they were first introduced not so many years ago. Summed up, what they consist in is an obligation not to keep personal information about individuals except in certain set circumstances, including the situation where you have got the individuals' permission. In practice, businesses, particularly small businesses, tend to give very little emphasis to data protection requirements, and they are something of a "sleeping giant" as far as enforcement is concerned. Try having a look at the information on the

GOV.UK website relating to the Information Commissioners' Office (ICO).

8. Fire Regulations

Again, obviously one that is only relevant if you have business premises pure and simple (rather than simply working at home). If you are concerned about whether you comply with fire regulations, ask someone from the fire brigade to visit and advise: although you will probably find you are putting your head in the lion's mouth by doing so!

9. Compulsory Insurance

We're all used to the fact that car insurance in compulsory by law, but there are other compulsory insurances as well, depending on the type of business. This includes employer's liability insurance if you have staff. Speak to an insurance broker to find out what your obligations are here.

10. Building Regulations

These are most likely to be relevant if you are having any alterations done to work (or indeed home) premises. Most builders have (or should have) more than a passing acquaintance with these, and certainly a Charterd Surveyor would have, for the more complex situations.

11. Industry–Specific Regulations

These are the bits of red tape which apply to your specific business. An example of this, for buy to let landlords, is the requirement to provide a gas safety certificate and certification of electrical installations. One way you can find out what that industry specific regulations are for your area of business is to join, or at least consult the website of, am organisation whose members are people running your sort of business. Most trades, professionals and businesses have such an organisation.

CHAPTER 7
VAT

Do you ever have that sort of dream where you wake up sweating? I had one the other day. I was walking along the road, minding my own business, when a supermarket delivery van overtook me on my walk and stopped in front of me, blocking the road. The delivery driver got out. He was a very big man, and to my astonishment (although things are less surprising in dreams) he had a loaded pistol which was pointed at me. "I've got a job for you", he said.

I remember bleating ineffectually that I didn't want a job, but the brute ignored me. He said "You see all those boxes in the back of my van? You're going to deliver them to that farmhouse over there. In my dream I could see the farmhouse was a long way away, across several fields, some of them very muddy and some ploughed. Another had a herd of cows with a very dangerous looking bull. The next thing I knew (the way one does in dreams) I found myself trudging across a field carrying a heavy box, and the delivery man's voice was close behind me. "Watch out for the landmines!"

"Why are there landmines here? and why don't you do this yourself?" I whined ineffectually.

"Because I put them there. And I'm too busy to do the delivery myself, so get on with it or you'll suffer."

Somehow in my dream, although the delivery man was a long way behind me by now, I knew that he was sitting in his van with his feet up on the steering wheel, reading the paper and smoking a fag. It seemed very unfair to me. Then I heard a bull running up behind me and I took to my heels, carrying the box which was spilling out bottles of fairy liquid and boxes of cornflakes as I tried to escape.

"You'll get into trouble for dropping those!" shouted the delivery man from the safety of his van.

The last thing I remember was the bull was chasing me directly towards a landmine. There was no way I could avoid it. Then I woke up.

Returning slowly to consciousness, I thought of the way the VAT system is set up (I am an accountant, after all). The government has imposed on those in business the job of being an unpaid tax collector; administering a system which is so complex that the paid officials themselves often get it wrong. And they impose draconian penalties on those who make any mistakes. So welcome to the modern world of business, and in particular of the system of VAT, introduced courtesy of what we were originally taught to call the Common Market, back in the early 1970's.

How VAT Works

The basic concept of VAT is simple. Businesses add a certain percentage on to their sales, which their customers have to pay them, which is tax due to the government. In order to make it a tax on the final consumer rather than on business as such (or this is the story they tell) businesses which receive supplies with this tax added to them are able to reclaim that tax, and only pay over to the government, therefore, effectively a tax on the value they add. The "fun" comes with the interpretation of the VAT rules setting out different rates of tax for different sorts of service. We put the word "fun" in inverted commas because VAT is one of the most tedious impositions, in reality, that business is faced with. Every quarter (or some businesses, every month) a return has to be submitted to HMRC – electronically – in which the VAT on sales (called "outputs") is added up, and the VAT on purchases and overheads ("inputs") are deducted from them, and the net result is a payment due to HMRC (or, in some cases, a repayment due to the business). Miles Kington (the late lamented comic writer) somewhere refers to "a person doing something with all the enthusiasm of a man sitting down to do his VAT return", and that is about the size of it.

The Good News

Our apologies for the very downbeat opening to this chapter on VAT, but, as we said right from the beginning, we're not trying to put positive spin on the realities of running a business: we're not trying to sell anything, just help people by telling it how it is. But the good news, particularly relevant to business start-up's, is that you don't have to sign on as an unpaid tax collector for the government straight away, or at all if your sales turnover, measured over an annual period, doesn't go over the VAT registration threshold. In the UK, we have the highest VAT threshold in Europe, which at the time of writing (2021) is annual turnover of £85,000.

And the second bit of good news is that not all business turnover is vatable. If you are in the type of business whose outputs are exempt, you don't need to register for VAT: indeed, if all of your sales are exempt, you're not even allowed to. If you have different sorts of supplies that you make in your business, some of which are exempt and some taxable, you only have to register if the taxable ones on their own exceed the registration threshold.

As a handy reference, we've included, as Appendix 2 to this book, a list of the various VAT categories: exempt, "zero rated" (of which more below), reduced rate supplies, and then there's the rest, which are fully taxable. So, for example, if your business is doing up and selling, or renting, "second hand" residential property, then all of your "outputs" are exempt, and there's no question of registering for VAT, and there are a whole host of other exempt categories including medical services, insurance and finance, education, etc. Have a look at Appendix 2 to see where your business supplies fall.

The Best of Both Worlds

If your supplies are zero rated, you've got what might be called the best of both worlds. Technically your turnover is taxable, but at a rate of zero percent. The big difference between this and being exempt from VAT is that zero rated businesses can reclaim the VAT on their purchases and expenses: so such businesses tend to receive repayments of VAT every quarter. In practice the most common examples of such VAT – favoured businesses are builders of new homes and supplies of food, like farmers, butchers and greengrocers, and so on.

Corner shops and the like tend to be in a more ambiguous position, because they will be selling both zero rated products (most food) and also standard rated, like alcoholic drinks and "luxury" items like sweets and chocolate. This used to be a real headache in the old days, separating out the sales between the VAT categories, when you might make hundreds of sales of different products every hour. Nowadays, most sensible shop keepers have electronic tills which separate out the different categories automatically.

VAT Record Keeping

As we said in Chapter 4, VAT registered businesses are now obliged to have their records on computer, and manual records aren't an option. This is under the infamous "Making Tax Digital" program. But non VAT registered businesses need not crow: Making Tax Digital is coming for anyone liable to income tax, with the current (at the time of writing) planned start date being 6 April 2023.

VAT Danger Areas

Whilst it would be fair to describe VAT as an extremely boring tax, it's also a tax which can be very expensive to get wrong. If mistakes are made in VAT accounting, these can cost the business (rather than the customers of the business, on whom VAT is meant to be a tax). Here are some of the pitfalls to watch out for:

- Unless you are going to register voluntarily for VAT at the outset (of which more below) it's sensible to wait until your business turnover has exceeded the registration threshold before registering; because in the interim, you will have a period of VAT free trading. But it's easy to miss the exact point at which you go over the threshold, and you only have a short time to react to this. Once your turnover has exceeded the threshold in the previous 12 monthly period (looking at it at the end of **each** month) you have until the end of the following month to notify your requirement to be registered to HMRC. Failure to do this will result in penalties. All too often, as accountants, we see that a client has gone over the limit in the period for which we have just received the books: which can sometimes be a period which is many months in the past.

- Sometimes a bookkeeper will claim VAT on expenses where there is no VAT actually included in them, like insurance or rent; or on which VAT reclaim is forbidden by specific rules, of which the principal examples are purchase of cars and entertaining expenditure. Because this tends to be a systemic error, made by the bookkeeper out of sheer ignorance, it can sometimes be repeated many times and add up to a significant amount of tax for HMRC to reclaim (with penalties) when they become aware of the situation. If you do notice errors of this kind, you may get out of penalties, though, by owning up yourself before the VATman finds out.

- It's important to appreciate that it is the person who is registered for VAT, and the not the business. So if the same individual, or the same combinations of persons in partnership, run more than one business, then VAT registration of one of those businesses means that all the others also need to be put through the VAT system.

- One of the most common VAT errors, again made by bookkeepers who aren't experts in the tax, is getting the rate of VAT wrong. This can actually work both ways. For example, we have quite often seen an example of a business charging VAT on rents charged for letting or subletting commercial premises. VAT doesn't apply to such rent **unless** the business has "opted to tax" the rents. Without such an option, such rents are exempt. On the other hand, a business might mistakenly zero rate a supply which is fully taxable. A common example of this is suppliers of food, who supply "in the course of catering". Food becomes vatable at the standard rate (currently 20%) when its supplied in this way; whereas food which is simply bought off a supermarket shelf, for example, will be zero rated. This kind of subtle distinction is often lost on those who are administering the VAT system for a business.

HMRC "Control" Visits

From time to time, if you're unlucky, the VATman will contact you to arrange a visit. It would be quite wrong to refer to visiting VAT officers as the "gestapo" or anything like that. As their published material makes clear, they're only interested in "helping" businesses to get their VAT right. But part of this help consists in the imposition of penalties (and interest) where a visiting officer, who is entitled at any reasonable time to make an appointment to come and look through your books, finds that you or your bookkeeper have got anything wrong, perhaps along the lines of one of the above danger areas. And this points to a major weakness in the way most businesses deal with their VAT obligations. Because it's boring, and administering it tends to consist of a lot of repetitive and fairly mindless inputting, the job naturally tends to descend to a fairly lowly individual within the business, who has no technical knowledge of the subject. So mistakes can easily arise, particularly in such a complicated system as VAT actually is. There are plenty of ploughed fields, landmines, and mad bulls in the VAT system despite its original proclamation as a "simple tax".

One way to cope with this is to get your accountant to do your VAT returns. In many cases, though, this may be seen as prohibitively expensive. As an alternative, you could consider having a "mock VAT visit". You ask your accountant (or an independent tax adviser) to visit and basically replicate what the gestapo (sorry, helpful HMRC officers) would do in the way of running through the books and records. In this way errors may be detected in time to put them right and avoid the effect multiplying over the future.

Voluntary Registration

What we have said up to now probably hasn't exactly "sold" the idea of VAT registration as a good thing for a business. But there are instances where businesses volunteer to register for VAT when they don't need to – because their vatable turnover is less than the threshold. Why would anyone be such a screwball?

To answer this, we need to go back to the basic concept of VAT. If vatable supplies are made by one business to another business, which itself is also VAT registered, that recipient business can reclaim all the VAT charged, and therefore it doesn't mind whether you are VAT registered or not: you are just as cheap as far as that customer business is concerned, as someone who isn't registered for VAT, even though you add 20% on to your sales invoices. Against this, being VAT registered, of course, means that you can reclaim the tax on your expenses and purchases. So whereas a business which is supplying members of the public, for example, who can't reclaim the VAT, will probably make less profit if they are registered (all other things being equal), because the non VAT registered customer will only pay what they think is reasonable for your goods or services, and won't pay any extra just because you're VAT registered, in the case of the business to business supplier your profit is increased to the tune of the amount of VAT you can reclaim on your inputs (minus the cost of operating VAT accounts when you don't need to).

CHAPTER 8
PROMOTION AND MARKETING

If you're the sort of reader who dips into a book rather than reading it from cover to cover, we have to say we have a lot of sympathy with you. With a book like this, you don't pick it up to enjoy our elegant turn of phrase, or to get lost in lengthy descriptions. The purpose of this book is to impart information, and the best way to do this, we think, is to make it short and punchy.

So on the subject of promotion and marketing, we've got quite a lot of ideas to put in front of you, as you'll see if you read on to the end of the chapter, but even if you pick up just two essential messages from a 30 second perusal of this chapter, we think we'll have done a good job.

So what is our essential two part message?

The first essential point is to abandon all traditional ideas of business promotion. In the memory of some of us who are not yet old, the way you promoted a business was by advertisements in newspapers and journals, and even on the radio or television. Those days are gone! Not only is advertisement on social media like Facebook, and online platforms like Amazon, more effective, it's infinitely more effective. The obvious fact of the matter is that anyone wanting to buy goods or services these days goes to the internet as a kind of "kneejerk" reaction. If this is not true in absolutely all businesses it is in the vast majority. So, forget ideas of a traditional advertising campaign and get to know how things are dealt with by successful online platforms. If your market is amongst professionals and senior business people, consider Linkedin: but be careful about giving any of these organisations a blank cheque book, as the computer can spend your money quite fast if you don't keep an eye on it.

Our other message is to beware of marketing specialists and consultants. Whilst these more often prey on larger and established businesses, they will certainly take your money if you decide to use their services. On the face of it, you might wonder, what could be more reasonable than going to a self-confessed expert in gathering new customers for your new business, when you, perhaps, start off by knowing little or nothing about how you're going to do this?

There are no doubt good and effective marketing consultants out there, but our experience suggests that those that you bring in from outside, sometimes at great expense, know little more than you do about your market, or perhaps know even less. Their stock in trade tends to be glib sayings like "Marketing is about how you answer the phone"; and often they will go into great detail in analysing the way the interior of your business should work – which is a comparatively easy and pleasant job for them to do – rather than the more "nitty gritty", and difficult, job of bringing new customers in through the door and laying them on the mat.

The more snooty members of the marketing "profession" make a big thing about how "sales" is different from "marketing". Indeed it is. Though it may be vulgar to say so, it's your down to earth salesman, not your high falutin marketing consultant, who brings in the real money.

Perhaps we've been unfortunate in our experience of "professional" marketers, but the root of the problem with trying to turn promotion and marketing into some kind of learned profession is that the marketing needs of different businesses are so different in themselves. What works for one business, even within the same industry, might not work for another; and between industries the whole approach to marketing can differ, if that marketing is to be successful.

You might say – with some reason – that we're queering our own pitch here, because if sales and marketing isn't the kind of universal expertise that can be learnt, but is purely a kind of "try it and see" exercise, then it follows that it's also not the kind of thing you can learn from a book. Our views are no doubt controversial, and some will be inclined strongly to disagree – particularly those who've written books on the subject, or those who make their living as marketing consultants. But we stand by them, because remember: we're not trying to sell anything ourselves, and we share between us an immense amount of practical experience in the real world of starting and running businesses.

So if we can't teach you how to sell your product in one easy lesson, what we can at least do is put some ideas down for you to think about. Many of these you will regard as fairly obvious, but others may give you pause for thought. The golden rule is that there is no golden rule. Not only can we say with confidence that not all these ideas will be relevant to all businesses, but we would go an awful lot further than that and say that very few of the ideas will be of relevance to any particular business, and in some cases, even, none of them might be. But you can only find out by thinking about it, and perhaps, in some cases, by trying it.

The Written Word

It's not true to say that you absolutely **have** to have a website. It depends on the type of business. For example, individual tradespeople like plumbers and electricians don't tend to have websites unless they have serious ambitions to become something more. The same could be said for specialist consultants, barristers etc whose reputation is already so good that they don't need any more clients, and couldn't cope with them if they had them. Why waste time and money on a website if you're this sort of one man/woman business? For the rest of us though, a website is pretty much a necessity these days. Have you not found yourself, as we have, skating over those businesses that don't have a website in search of one that does, when you're surfing the net looking for a product or service?

As well as an individual business website, it's obviously a good idea to get on to any kind of register of businesses of a similar type that there may be. And there are umbrella websites for these, like Checkatrade.com, and others. To some extent these sites are the modern equivalent of the late lamented Yellow Pages. But many times more powerful than these is the mighty leviathan called Google. It's a fact of life that people rarely scroll beyond the first page or two, when searching for a particular type of business, and therefore a lot of time and ingenuity is given to trying to get one's own website high up on the google list. This is given the grand title of SEO, or Search Engine Optimisation. Some people are apparently experts in it, but if you can't afford a SEO expert, consider these one or two key features, which by common consent are meant to improve your position in the google rankings:

- Put plenty of interesting content on the site, using a lot of different words to mean similar things, with the aim of picking up on key word searches;
- Put in as many links as possible to other sites; and
- Change your content regularly, perhaps by including a "blog".

And don't forget to visit your own website often. There are things which will leap out at you, when you see it as it were from the customer's eye view, that you may have missed when actually providing the original content for the site.

Whilst on the subject of the written word, (and picture) try inserting "advertorial" in newspapers and magazines that are read by potential customers. You know the sort of thing:

From Manufacturing Weekly:

Tough Times Ahead for Plastic Extrusion Moulding

The challenges of Brexit and the Covid Pandemic are set to put a lot of PEM companies out of business according to Jeff Vinyl, MD of specialist PEM firm Celluloid Contours Limited of Reading. The inability to move with the times and produce innovative and cheap solutions for manufacturers seeking plastic parts will turn these companies into a generation of dinosaurs. In times when most PEM businesses are laying off staff, Jeff's company is bucking the trend: with a new factory planned to open up in Woking next Spring and significant investment in computer technology which will enable bespoke products to be produced at the click of a mouse at the fraction of the cost ...

And so on. Not all editors are that favourable to thinly disguised advertising of this sort, but many will just be grateful for something to fill in the space on their regular publications.

More ambitiously, if you are an expert or professional, writing and publishing a book is a clear sign that you know what you're talking about (or don't, as the case may be!).

Personal Contact

However much the less outgoing amongst us might shy away from it, there's nothing to beat personal contact for some types of business, as a method of drumming up custom. Again this will be in different spheres depending on the type of business. In some sorts of business you will get customers from joining elite organisations, like the Freemasons or "gentlemen's" clubs. Being heart and soul in following a particular sport will also get you clients or customers, and although we wouldn't suggest you counterfeit interest in something that bores you, there's no doubt that some types of sport are more effective than others, depending on the type of client/customer you want. So typically, we find, rugby can be better than football from this point of view, and golf better than tennis.

Then there are mutual services. This can be particularly helpful for professionals, who can build up a kind of "local mafia" who always try to refer their clients to each other. If you're a lawyer and have recommended your friend who is an accountant to a client, the friend will almost certainly reciprocate by sending you one of his clients when they have legal work that needs doing. The lunch table is an excellent place for building up these local mafia relationships. This principle can be useful even in what seem like non business situations. When your dentist or doctor asks you how you are, lead the conversation on to your business. It's amazing how often they or someone they know will be interested in becoming a client or customer of the business.

Sometimes (with a heavy emphasis on that word) having a stall at a trade fair might pick up customers.

But, still on the subject of personal contact, as we said earlier on in this chapter, employing, or going into partnership with, a good salesman or woman who knows what he or she is doing is by far the most effective way of increasing your turnover in some types of business. You might be the most skilled and expert plastic extrusion moulder the world has ever known, at the same time as being a terrible ambassador for your product. Sales, and making the things that are sold, are two completely different skills. And, as we say, it's those with the first skill who make all the money in this world.

Customer Friendly

Bear in mind that it's easy to overlook how your product or service, and your business generally, actually comes over to the customers. We're definitely not suggesting bombarding customers with "surveys" until they wish they never heard your name. But a very little bit of business introspection can sometimes reveal areas where dealing with you is an unpleasant or irritating experience for the people you're wanting to make money from.

In some sorts of business, too, consider whether competitive pricing, free samples, and customer incentives like two for one offers might help bring you the repeat business that is so important.

The Brand

A lot of nonsense is talked, in our experience, about brand, by those who set themselves up as marketing experts. In some types of business, particularly professional services, the brand is actually of no importance whatever in the real world. But other types of business – and yours may be one – do benefit from having an eye catching name, logo, or colour scheme. For example, if you're running a taxi firm, consider how important the colour scheme could be. The yellow cab in New York, and the Black Cab in London, are icons. So why not flood a town with bright orange cars, with an easily memorable phone number on the side, and see how this marks you out above your competition? You don't have to be any better than the competition, or even different from them. You just need, in these types of businesses, to have a memorable public image.

And don't forget the importance of repetition. You may find that the same person ignores the first, second, and third time they come across you, by whatever means. But the fourth or fifth time the same simple message makes itself felt, they might well buy.

The Unique Selling Point

In marketing jargon, it is the USP. This isn't particularly a sales or marketing point, however. It's more about what fundamentally makes your business likely to succeed or not. The taxi firm with the bright orange cars doesn't really have a USP in the proper sense, because the service they provide is exactly the same as that of all the other taxi firms. But a taxi firm that provides a free gin and tonic with every ride would have a USP. That particular example, of course, is a flippant one, and perhaps we should also warn of the dangers of gimmickry. A gimmick does help attract customers in many sorts of industry, no doubt; but they are customers who won't stay long unless you either change the gimmick or have a particularly excellent product. And this brings us on to the most screamingly obvious way there is of promoting your business and increasing sales. It begins with a "Q".

Quality

We call it obvious, but if it were as obvious as all that, we wouldn't see so many businesses demonstrably failing, in a big way, to tap into this sure fire method of business expansion. If you're a restaurant, and you send away customers with a poor meal, after an inordinate wait, you may be unaware of those customers choosing never to come again. You'll just be puzzled as to why business doesn't seem to be so good as in the other restaurant at the other side of town. We've already talked about the things which turn would be repeat customers off. But don't forget that it's not just about looking good, but being good. If you turn out a product of excellent quality, you won't just get those repeat customers, but you'll get everyone else they recommend your business to. And think carefully about what the word "excellent" actually means. It's often used fairly vaguely to mean the same as "very good", but what it literally means is that you are better than someone else.

We do apologise to those readers who are tapping their fingers impatiently, whilst we labour this point, which should be obvious. But, as we say, it seems to be a lesson that a high proportion of those in business haven't actually yet learnt.

CHAPTER 9

CHOOSING AND USING ACCOUNTANTS AND OTHER ADVISERS

You will have found, if you've looked, that there's no shortage of advice on offer for business start-ups. And that includes this book, of course! But it's getting the right advice that is the really difficult thing. In this chapter we'll be telling you the sort of advisers to choose, and the sort to avoid (almost as important); how to spot the key differences between useful advisers and the other sort; and, which is quite likely to be an immediately pressing issue: how to find a good accountant.

Those Who Can, Do. Those Who Can't, Teach

This well known saying, attributed to George Bernard Shaw and no doubt others, is certainly true in the sphere of business advice. There seem to be a lot of people out there who haven't made any conspicuous success in business themselves, but have set up to advise or "coach" others. As we said in the introduction to this book, a successful business is much more likely to be a passport to wealth than teaching others to run their businesses; and you may wonder why, therefore, many of these advisers or business coaches aren't practising what they preach, but instead are spending their scarce resource of time giving away business secrets to all and sundry. The key question which all of these people should be asked (but aren't always) is: If you're so good at knowing how to run a business, why don't you spend your time doing that instead of talking to us? It's very rare, in our experience, that they have a convincing answer to this question.

But what about this book, you might say? Well, we started off by saying that we weren't trying to sell anything: except this book. Having built up a successful business ourselves (providing tax advice and accountancy services) our business itself is advising others, and the book virtually writes itself – because it's based almost exclusively on our practical experience of actually setting up and running businesses. Most of those who buy this book won't be business rivals of ours in any sense, and writing a book based on your experience is an enjoyable diversion from the ordinary business of running our practice from day to day.

Whom to Avoid

We'd like to apologise in advance to the "good" exponents of the disciplines that we're about to mention. If you're a business coach, for example, with a track record of measurably increasing your clients' profits to a significant degree, the remarks that follow aren't addressed to you, and we apologise if we are tarring you with the same brush as the other sort. But in our experience, the not so good ones tend to be in a majority in the areas that follow.

So, particularly in the sensitive and cash strapped start-up period of your business, avoid:

- Business coaches. This is not a recognised profession, although no doubt someone will have set up an "Institute of Business Coaches" or the like. The stock in trade of what you might call your average business coach is dressing up the obvious as though it were a tremendous revelation. For example, if you are producing manufactured goods, changing the components so that on average they are cheaper will add to your profit. Doing market research will enable you to identify potential customers. Cutting your overheads will increase your bottom line profit; and so on. A business coach is often someone who will talk to you about your business, and regurgitate what you yourself have told him in a glossy report, and then send in his bill. Or he will be on a retainer, employed on a regular income to read back your accounting numbers to you (useful, we suppose, if you don't understand accounts yourself and there's an element of interpretation involved).

- Mentor courses. These are people who've discovered that you can make quite a lot of money setting up as a guru, and giving courses (mostly online these days). At the business start-up stage, and still more in the period before you start-up, you're in no position, frankly, to judge whether such courses are worth the money you have to pay to go on them. The bad ones feed on the natural diffidence of would-be business owners as to their own skills and aptitude for entrepreneurship. Actually, the only way you're going to find out whether you are cut out for business is trying it. And ask yourself, in the case of a few well known successful tycoons, whether it's likely that they got there as a result of going on courses.

- Marketing experts. We've already had a go at these in Chapter 8; but in case you skipped that, we'll give you the benefit of our own experience in using marketing experts, when we were trying to use this "artificial" means of increasing the scale of our accountancy practice. Our experience was basically that they were more interested in an analysing the way the business works, and the attitudes of the owners and staff to each other and the business, and feeding this back, than actually getting down to the nitty gritty of telling us how to attract new clients. One well known marketing guru told all the members of a medium sized accountancy firm that, when asked at parties what they did, they should answer "I turn dreams into reality." We had a good chuckle about the sublime fatuity of that; but the smile turns a little bit sour when one gets a bill for this sort of advice. As we've already pointed out, it's not the marketers of this world who make the big money: it's the salesman and women. That's our experience, and marketers themselves are always very quick to highlight the difference between marketing (which is a kind of superior, professional activity) and "mere" sales. But it's the vulgar salesman that you see driving around in the top of the range Mercedes.

- Advisers from the bank. Possibly most pointless of all are those who are part of the bank, or who are approved advisers of the bank, coming to tell you how to run your business. Whatever superb and useful qualities working in a bank imparts to these professionals, knowledge of how business actually works and what makes it succeed is not one of them.

The Good Guys

So we haven't minced our words about these advisers who, with the exception of the (we think very few) good ones, generally just tend to act as a parasite on a business. This may all sound hopelessly cynical; but remember that the authors of this book have got over half a century of experience, between them, of running businesses in the real world!

Another attack that might be made on our whole approach here is to say: "We notice that you haven't had a go at the accountancy profession, as yet? Could that be anything to do with the fact that you're accountants yourselves?"

Don't worry: our cynicism extends to our own profession as well! We will be talking about how to find a good accountant shortly. But it's worth pointing out, before moving on to that, that accountants' advice is typically far more concrete and less "airy fairy" than your business coach or your marketing expert. This is because they deal at the "coalface" with the actual financial results of business, and money, after all, is the purpose and the lifeblood of business.

But who should you listen to, apart from accountants? Most entrepreneurs and would-be business people are control freaks, and actually they don't feel they need to take advice from anyone. This is a common failing, and a reason for businesses failing as well. But it's the flip side of the self confidence and the ability to make firm decisions which is an essential part of the DNA of the successful business person. Such people listen to their accountants, and try and get as much juice as possible from the accountant's input. But their tendency to take advice elsewhere is, in practice, usually limited to talking to other business people, who have successfully, perhaps, negotiated the same sort of problematical teething problems that the budding entrepreneur is now facing. So, if you're fortunate enough to know somebody who has been successful in business, tap into them mercilessly. If they've been successful, most of them will have a weakness, indeed, for boasting about their success and the decisions they made to get them there. You can, and should, take these with a pinch of salt; but you'll undoubtedly learn a lot from soaking in the "atmosphere" of a successful person's reminiscences: the blend of decisiveness, ruthlessness, and courage which make up a successful man or woman of action.

Choosing an Accountant

If you're an accountant yourself (and lots of those starting up in business furnish themselves with this training before doing so: an excellent plan in most cases) you may not feel the need to take accountancy advice at the start-up stage of the business. Everyone else, though, will probably be well advised to get an accountant on board at an early a stage. But we probably ought, at this point, to be careful about defining our terms. This is because the meaning of the term "accountant" has subtly but definitely changed over the last 30 years or so.

In the 1980's, it was still generally true to say that, if you had a tax problem, or wanted tax planning advice, you went to your accountant. But times have changed since then. The whole of UK direct tax legislation could be printed in a single volume in those days, printed on thick paper. Nowadays, no fewer than six such volumes come out each year, printed on thin paper. So tax (which has always been part of the accountant's core service) is something like ten times as complicated now as it was 30 years ago. The result is that for anything other than the most basic tax advice (for example, how to comply with your HMRC obligations, and what the tax rates and thresholds are) you need to go to a practitioner of a comparatively new profession: that of tax adviser. Although almost all accountancy firms have a tax partner or tax manager so called, generally speaking this doesn't connote expertise in tax planning; more often it's simply expertise in doing the tax returns for individual and company clients after the event – a very different discipline. So that's our first lesson for you in the area of choosing and using an accountant. Be quite clear what the difference is between an accountant and a tax adviser.

Narrowing the Choice

Just like when you're choosing an estate agent, there no doubt seem to be hundreds of firms out there, all pretty much indistinguishable, making it more like closing your eyes and putting a pin in a copy of the yellow pages than any rationally informed choice. But there are a couple of pointers, which we hope will radically narrow the field for you, in what follows.

First of all, how big is the firm? For business start-up's, we're very much of the view that "small is beautiful". Both the authors of this book have had experience of working in very large, very small, and "medium sized" accounting practices, and our experience of the large firm is that they are very unlikely to be well geared up to providing a useful service for the brand new or embryo business. This isn't having a go at them in any way; it's just not what they tend to be good at. The large firms tend to be geared towards dealing with large clients, particularly publicly quoted groups of companies, and their directors. Typically, if you take on one of the "big four" or "big twelve", you will have different people dealing with different aspects of your business, with the tax department dealing with your tax and the accounting/audit with your accounts; and very often these two departments don't even talk to each other. Whilst a lot of these firms pay lip service to an "integrated" service for the smaller business, their hearts don't tend to be in it, in our experience. And, very often, a large firm will mean large bills.

Medium sized firms come in a number of sub-categories,

from the nationwide firms which are really just like the large firms on a slightly smaller scale; and the local firms who are like a lot of small firms leagued together. The latter can have the advantage of there being central expertise available which wouldn't be available to a small local firm or sole practitioner. In particular this might be the case with the trickier tax problems, where a medium sized firm might be big enough to have a specialist tax adviser on board. But even the very small firm or sole practitioner has access to this kind of adviser, albeit on a freelance external basis. And the merit of the small firm, which some will consider the supreme merit in these situations, is that they are sometimes (but not always) very cheap!

We know from experience that there's no such thing as a "market rate" for accountancy services. Bills come in all shapes and sizes, with apparently comparable firms charging amounts which differ from each other by a multiple of two or even three.

"Specialists"

If you have issues in your situation which might make tax important (for example if the VAT rules applying to your type of business are complex, or you are undertaking tax favoured research and development – or even if you've got some inherited tax problem) then choose a firm, if you can find one, with demonstrable tax expertise. The problem, here, is that all accountancy firms claim to have this: but the ones which actually have it will tend to be distinguished clearly even on their websites, as having dedicated tax advisory partners; and perhaps will also write their own materials on tax, for the website and elsewhere.

But there's another type of purported "specialism" that you should beware of. Sometimes a firm will say that it is a specialist in your particular field of business or industry. This is no doubt excellent PR for these firms, because if you are in the business of plastic extrusion moulding, and you see someone who claims to be a specialist in the accounting for plastic extrusion moulding, you will feel that you are going to some one good. But the reality of the matter is that there is no fundamental difference in the way that most different businesses are accounted for, and charged to tax. Plastic extrusion moulding is like any other kind of manufacturing process in reality, as far as the skills that it calls for in an external accountant are concerned. There are some genuine specialisms, however, where you will be starting that much ahead of the game if you choose an accountant who is demonstrably skilled and experienced in that area (remember the axiom that one client in a given industry makes an accountant an "expert", and two makes him a "specialist"). These include:

- Insurance Companies;
- Law Firms (where there are stringent requirements with regarding to the accounting for clients' money);
- Travel Agents (because of their nightmare VAT arrangements);
- Pharmacists (again because of their complex VAT accounting);
- International Entertainers and Sportsmen;
- Import and Export Businesses; and
- Offshore Based Businesses.

If you feel you have a business with specialist accounting requirements, and are considering appointing a particular firm, ask whether they have experience in this area or whether they feel that specialist experience is necessary. It may be by no means obvious from their website whether they have this expertise or not, so take nothing for granted.

Word of Mouth

Traditionally the best way of finding a good accountant, or indeed any professional, is by word of mouth. If you have friends in business, ask who their accountant is and whether they rate them. If you haven't any friends in this position, consider asking your solicitor, who inevitably will have had dealings with most of the accountants round about. Or even your banker, if you're fortunate to have a banking relationship with an individual, as used to be the case. Bankers, though, whilst they used to be a prime referral source for new clients for the accountancy profession, very rarely recommend firms these days.

The Practicalities of Appointing an Accountant

One thing that has changed comparatively recently is that geography is no longer anything like so much of an issue. Our own accountancy firm is based in Tunbridge Wells, in Kent. But we have clients the length and breadth of Great Britain, and in Northern Ireland, none of whom seem to find the relationship a difficult one because of the physical distance. The reason for this, of course, is the speed and ease of modern communication, with accounting records being directly accessible remotely, and communication being instantaneous. As a general principle, we would say that it's much more important to have the right accountant for you than to have one who is situated conveniently nearby.

Finally, on the practicalities, you may well feel disinclined to give your accountant a "blank chequebook" as has traditionally been the custom. Accountants are used, these days, to being asked for a quotation in advance for their costs.

CHAPTER 10
STRUCTURING A BUSINESS TAX EFFICIENTLY

When it comes to how you structure your new enterprise you've got a choice, essentially, between four different business vehicles, if you ignore the very rare ones like trusts and foundations. What you choose now, at the outset of the business, can make a huge amount of difference to the tax you pay, so this chapter should be required reading for any business start-up.

What is the best and most tax efficient structure to set up a new business in, then?

The answer to this question, unfortunately, isn't the same in all cases. It depends very much on the situation, and in particular the amount and timing of the profits you anticipate. But so that you can make an informed decision on which of the structures to choose, we'd best go through them in a certain amount of detail.

The simplest form of business structure is the sole tradership. That is a single individual carrying on the business in his or her own name. The profits that a sole tradership business makes are chargeable to income tax, directly on the individual, and it makes no difference whether the individual leaves those profits in the business bank account or draws them out and spends them privately. As far as red tape is concerned, there is the least of all of this unpleasant and counterproductive commodity in a sole tradership business. You don't have to prepare accounts to any particular format: the only requirement, imposed for tax purposes, is that they should give a true and fair view of your profit for the year. Also, the accounts don't have to be published anywhere: they are a matter between you and your taxman (and possibly also bank manager).

Next up in our ascending sequence of business structures is the general, or unincorporated partnership. We say "unincorporated" because you don't have to do anything positive or definite in order to create a partnership. The relationship just comes into being whenever two or more people carry on a business in common and share the profits. If you want to add formality to the arrangements, you can have a written partnership agreement, which sets out such matters as how the profits are divided, who decides whether drawings of money are made out of the business bank account, and generally who runs the show. But a partnership agreement isn't a legal requirement at all. It can even be a purely verbal agreement, for example to the effect that Partner A has two thirds of the profits and Partner B has one third, and so on. But if there isn't actually any agreement, either written or verbal, then the law is that the profits are shared equally, and people have equal voting rights. Like a sole tradership, a partnership is not subject to any legal requirements as to the format under which it prepares its accounts and also like a sole tradership the accounts don't have to be published. As with a sole tradership, the partners are taxed directly on the business profits whether they draw them out of the business bank account in cash or other forms, or not. The tax is a direct liability of each partner, calculated based on the share of profits attributed to that partner, taxed at whatever that partner's marginal tax rate is.

The third type of business vehicle that is commonly used is a more recent addition to the collection. This is the Limited Liability Partnership, first introduced into UK law by the Limited Liability Partnerships Act 2000. In some ways, the name "partnership" is a misnomer, because a Limited Liability Partnership, or LLP, is actually a body corporate legally, like a limited company. But for tax purposes (which is what this chapter is mainly about) it's treated, by a kind of legal fiction, as if it were a partnership. In practical terms the difference between an LLP and a general unincorporated partnership is firstly that, as the name suggests, partners (called members in an LLP) have limited liability. So if things go horribly wrong for the business, and it goes bust, the individual members are in a similar position to the shareholders in a company: all they lose is the amount they have invested in the LLP, and creditors of the LLP can't normally (in the absence of things like personal guarantees or personal negligence) go against the private assets of the members. Secondly, an LLP's accounts do have to be prepared in accordance with a format strictly laid down in the law, and the accounts, together with details of the membership of the LLP, have to be placed on public record at Companies House. If you like, you can think of these formalities and disclosure requirements as part of the "price" of trading with limited liability. As with sole traders and partnerships, the tax applies directly to the member, on his her or its share of profits. There's no difference to the tax, again, whether the profits are drawn out of the business or left in.

Finally, we come to the structure that most people tend to begin with: the Limited Company. Like an LLP a limited company is a body corporate legally, which means it is treated as if it were its own separate person, with the capacity to own assets, enter into contracts, and generally run a business on its own account. Also like an LLP, a limited company provides limited liability to its shareholders, and has strict accounting and public disclosure requirements. Unlike all of the other structures we've been talking about, though, the limited company has its own tax liability on its profits. This is corporation tax rather than income tax, and tends to be historically at a lower rate than income tax, at least over a certain fairly low level of total income. It follows that, also unlike the other three types of structure, it does make a difference to the tax payable whether or not profits are drawn out of the business or left in there. Profits drawn out from a company in the form of dividends are chargeable to income tax, meaning that those profits effectively bear two levels of tax: first at the company level (corporation tax) and then at the individual level (income tax). These two key factors, that corporation tax is generally lower than income tax, and that two layers of tax apply to money drawn out of the business, are key in deciding what business structure is the best for you in your business start-up.

A Common Myth

It's a common myth that a company is more tax efficient than a sole tradership or partnership etc. There are situations where it is, and situations where it's quite the reverse.

Take John for example. He has enough income from sources other than the business to put him into higher rates of income tax (40%), and he has the choice whether to run his new business as a company or a sole trader. If the profits are say £100,000, and John draws them all out of the business each year, the tax under the company route will first of all be corporation tax on the £100,000 profits, which at a 19% rate (the rate applying at time we are writing this) gives a corporation tax bill of £19,000. The company is therefore left with £81,000 to pay out as a dividend, which it duly does to John as the sole shareholder. John's personal income tax on this is £26,325. So John has, out of his £100,000 profits, £54,675 left after the two layers of tax. By running that same business as a sole trader, he would instead have 40% tax and 2% national insurance (again at the rates current at the time of writing), meaning that the total tax bill is £42,000 and he has £58,000 left after tax.

What makes this sort of decision so complicated is that there are so many different rates of tax and, indeed, national insurance. There's no substitute for actually doing the numbers in each case, or rather asking your accountant to if you're not that way inclined yourself.

Losses

Then there's the different way that the various structures deal with start-up losses. It's important to remember, here, that losses can result just from normal expenses exceeding income (which is quite likely in the early stages of any business), but losses can also be created by special tax allowances. For example, if you buy a new van, the chances are that, even if this is a permanent asset that you will be able to use for several years, you will be given a 100% tax write off for the cost of buying the van in your first period. The same applies to all kinds of plant and equipment purchased by a business. So it's important to be aware of the different way that start-up losses are treated between the different structures.

On the one side of the fence, as in so many things, you have partnerships, sole traders, and LLP's and on the other side of the fence you have limited companies. If you form a company to run your business from the word go, and it incurs tax losses, generally all you will be able to do with those losses is carry them forward and use them against profits that you hope the company will make from the trade in the future. The situation is quite different for the other sorts of business structure, where the losses are attributed directly (in the same way as profits are) to the individual partners or the sole trader. This loss can then be used to offset, for tax purposes, against other income received by those individuals, and perhaps achieve a very useful tax refund. In the early years of the business, indeed, there is an additional relief which consists in the ability to "carry back" the losses three years to periods which can be long before you started the business. So if, for example, you were a highly paid PAYE employee before you started the business, using a sole trader-ship, partnership, or LLP structure will enable you to tap into this very useful source of tax refunds.

When is a Limited Company Better?

We've already illustrated, in the case of John above, that a company doesn't actually save you tax, and can even cost you more tax, in situations where you simply pay all of the profits out to yourself as the shareholders. But of course this isn't always the way things happen.

Many kinds of business do better if profits, instead of being paid out to the business owners and "blown", so to speak, are ploughed back into the business. This is the case, for example, with businesses which do better if they hold more stock, or businesses which have work in progress on various projects. The more you plough the profits back, the larger scale your business becomes and, hopefully, the more profitable (although there is always the danger of "overtrad-ing" to consider – of which more later on in this book). So if profits are not actually paid out, but left in the business to form working capital, or even purchase fixed assets, then it makes sense for those retained profits only to have borne tax at the lower corporation tax rates. If you take a very typical situation where the company rate on profits would be 19% and the individual rate would be 40% on the same level of profits, running the business through a company means that you have 81% of your profits left, after tax, to reinvest, rather than only 60% which you would have going down the sole trader, partnership etc route.

We're beginning to get into more advanced levels of tax planning here, but it's also true to say that a company is a more tax efficient structure for a business where profits are paid out, but not paid out in income form. The following example illustrates a situation where this might be the case.

Stephanie decides to turn her substantial Victorian country house into a hotel. She confidently expects high levels of profits because of the beautiful setting of the property. On advice, therefore, she forms a limited company and transfers the property to the company in exchange for a director's loan account balance in her favour of the books of the company. Assuming that the property is worth £2 million, she therefore starts with the company owing her £2 million for the property. All goes well, the guests arrive, the weddings are booked, and the profits start rolling in. If, say, her profits are £100,000 in a year, how much tax does she have to pay on the basis that she takes all of the profits out to spend on her personal lifestyle?

The answer, here, is £19,000 (again using the 19% corporation tax rate that applies at the time of writing). There's no "double charge to tax" in this situation, because the company, having paid its corporation tax of £19,000 on the £100,000 profits, then uses the £81,000 it has left to repay some of the amount it owes Stephanie on director's loan account. She therefore has £81,000 after tax rather than the £58,000 that she would have had if she had operated the hotel as a sole trader.

You see what we mean about the advice being different in different situations. And we should make the point that, for the sake of simplicity, we haven't taken the promised future rate of 25% corporation tax for higher profits, announced in the 2021 Budget, into account in our examples; nor, in Stephanie's example, the possibility of Stamp Duty Land Tax having to be paid as part of the cost of incorporation.

If there is any kind of "safe" or "default" advice to give generally, though, it would be not to rush into forming a limited company unless the business presents high levels of risk from the outset (in which case an LLP might also be a good alternative). It is quite easy, in fact, to convert a business like a sole tradership or partnership into a limited company later if it turns out that the profits are at a level sufficient to justify the additional formality. (It isn't, incidentally, so easy to go the other way, from the limited company back to sole trader/partnership.) So it's probably sensible, if you don't really know how things are going to pan out with the business, to start off in a simple structure like a sole tradership or partnership. If you do, in fact, notch up tax losses, so much the better: these can be relieved in the way we've described. And you have the advantage of the much lower levels of formality in an unincorporated business. If then, as we say, profits turn out to be both high and of the sort that should be ploughed back into the business, transfer the business by all means at that stage to a limited company.

To find out more about this issue, and indeed tax planning in general, do have a look at Alan Pink's book Practical Tax Planning for Businesses which gives you a lot more detailed information than is possible or appropriate here.

CHAPTER 11
CONTROLLING OVERHEADS

There's always a danger of stating the ******** obvious, when someone sits down to write a chapter about controlling overheads. OK, this is a necessary (though boring) discipline for anyone who wants to build up a successful business. But you don't need to waste your time reading statements like "change your energy supplier to the cheapest provider" or "cutting your tea-breaks by 50% will save pounds on tea bags and sugar". Although there is an element of the obvious in all this – because income minus expenses equals profit – we think you may find quite a lot of what follows to be counter-intuitive. Let's start with the attitude of mind that says "we'd walk a mile in tight shoes to save a penny."

You would have thought that, being accountants, we would be all in favour of applying rigorous and constant downward pressure to expenditure. But as accountants who are actually running our own businesses as well, we're very much alive to the threat of the False Economy.

Beware False Economy

What's the man who walks a mile in tight shoes to save a penny neglecting to do, so that he can make this petty saving? In a business start-up situation, the person who's likely to be sitting on the phone, endlessly on hold to various call centres, to change his energy or broadband supplier to someone who is a few pounds less a month, is likely to be you. As the protagonist in the business, you're also the person on whom it depends to drive it forward. Your overhead savings, if you manage to make them, will need to be pretty massive to make up for the loss of your time, assuming your time is productive. (We'll come on to say more about the distinction between productive and non productive costs very shortly.)

Even if the person charged with reducing overheads in this obvious way is not a directly productive member of staff, if the exercise is diverting his or her attention away from doing something which will help to bring income in, it's very likely to be a false economy. In summary, what we're preaching here is the need to recognise the value of time. The value of time isn't what it actually costs you – which is zero, in one sense, if it's your own time as business owner – but what economists call the "opportunity cost" of not doing something else which could bring in income.

Productive and Non Productive Costs

Most of us, even those without a background in accounts, have at least an inkling of this all important distinction. The very word "overheads" carries with it an implication that costs which are described thus are pretty much fixed, and don't go up or down with the level of the business' turnover (sales). An example is the rent of your premises, if you occupy specific business premises. This won't go up and down as the level of business goes up and down, because you can't just occupy slightly more or slightly less in the way of premises. Insurance can be another example of such a cost. But what's important isn't the distinction between costs which are fixed and those which vary, but between those costs which are productive and those which are non productive. The reason this is important is that some costs, which fall to be described as "overheads" can actually be productive ones; such that cutting them risks cutting your ability to produce, and earn income. Let's look at a couple of examples.

Flog-it and Cash-in is a newly set up firm of estate agents. Jeff Flog-it and Bill Cash-in left a much larger firm in order to set up on their own, and they've got very clear ideas about the way they are going to do things better than their old firm. For a start, they decide, they're not going to have an army of junior individuals sitting around in the office, mostly filing their nails or looking at their phones, but are going to cut their "front of house" staff down to the bare minimum.

As a result, there are long periods where people phoning up the agency don't get an immediate answer to their calls. OK, they're asked to leave messages which Jeff, Bill or their part time assistant answers as soon as they get to them: but one or two of those ringing up are impatient types, and tell their friends not to go to this new agency. How many sales have been lost as a result of this penny pinching attitude? The answer is: no one can ever know, but it's very likely indeed to exceed, in value, the cost of employing some-body to look after the very important "front of house" function.

Although we've used the example of estate agents here, this same principle applies to almost any kind of business. In recent years, in fact, we've seen a huge explosion of this phenomenon, of businesses mounting formidable barriers in the way of anyone trying to communicate with them. This applies to businesses both small and big: think of the "call centre" phenomenon which makes it so difficult to communicate with a business, even when you want to pay them money. On the small end of the scale, which you will probably fall into as a start-up business, one of the last things you want to do is skimp in any way on your front of house facility - whatever form that takes in the particular circumstances of your business.

And returning to the cost accountancy formulation, think hard about how you classify the wages of that extra person you employ to answer the phone: productive or non productive?

Here's another example:

Gimme and Partners is a newly set up wealth management company. What they do is to take over the management of sums of money lodged with them by clients, in the hope that the value of the investments may sometimes go up as well as down. Gordon Gimme, the main man, has spent an awful lot of time and money setting up the firm, including the very onerous requirements of registering with the Financial Conduct Authority. His financial model is to run the business almost entirely "on the hoof": that is, he goes to see clients in his second-hand Audi A6, rather than inviting them to come to a plushly appointed office: and he and his two assistants "work from home".

In fact he's even bullish enough to try out, as an experiment, running the business without any premises at all, and using his home address as the registered office.

Very soon it becomes evident that this isn't practicable. A substantial enough proportion of clients want to come and see him, rather than the other way round. So, in a move which he hopes will please his accountant, he takes on a tiny office above a fish and chip shop in the cheap part of town. On the floor are offcuts of carpet, and the furniture is of the sort where the plastic veneer peels after the first few weeks of use. Gordon reckons that the few clients who do insist on coming to his office will tend to be of the sort, like Stephen Small, whom he doesn't need to impress with any kind of flashy presentation. But Gordon is unaware of the conversation that Stephen Small has with his maternal uncle Peter Bigg, a couple of days after his visit to Gordon's office.

"Oh, you wouldn't want to put your money with my guy," *Stephen says dismissively. "He's fine for the tuppence ha'penny I have to invest, but you need someone more professional for your £20 million."*

So what category does the expenditure on the office and presentation generally, fall into: productive or non productive?

We don't need to labour the point any further. Far from advocating a ruthless hatchet job on all of the business' overheads, we are sounding a warning not to strangle the goose that lays the golden egg. In some of the higher end "luxury" type services, which includes the more highfalutin type of "consultancy", the type of furniture you have in your reception and boardroom, the make of chocolate biscuits that are served up in meetings, and the quality of the tea and coffee, to say nothing of the location of your offices, can make a difference of more than 100% to the fee you can charge clients for providing exactly the same service. In making the all important distinction between productive and non productive expenses, think very hard about which is actually which.

Premises

Having made what we think is a very important point of principle, let's move the discussion on to a much more practical level. Our example of Gordon Gimme illustrates a type of business where the premises are important, and skimping on this expense is something you do at your peril. But for a lot of business start-ups, perhaps even the majority, running the business from home is perfectly possible and, if possible, is what you might call a complete no brainer. A large proportion of the overheads of any business (using the term overheads in its proper sense) will relate to the cost of maintaining business premises. So working from home can easily make a business viable that wouldn't have been if you had done it the old fashioned way and set up in an office/warehouse/factory in the town.

Some businesspeople are concerned about the tax effect of turning their house or flat into the HQ of a business. For example, do you have to pay business rates? Does using your house for a business mean that when, eventually, you sell it, you have to pay capital gains tax?

We're pleased to say that, in almost all cases, these tax based concerns are likely to be groundless. What is sometimes referred to as the "kitchen table business", where you don't generally see clients or customers at home, is unlikely to be taken into account for business rates purposes as such. And you can avoid paying CGT on the sale of your house etc by ensuring that no single part of the property is used **exclusively** for purposes of the business. Partial private use of your office at the bottom of the garden, for example, however occasional, is sufficient to avoid losing the CGT exemption which normally applies to the disposal of one's main residence.

And then there's the whole vexed question of working at home (or "from" home as it's more often, and rather mysteriously, termed these days). We call this a vexed question because, following the Covid crisis, the proportion of people working from home, and rarely if ever setting foot inside the business premises, has massively increased, It's a vexed question because this happened perforce, because people were afraid of getting ill: and so the pluses and minuses of a number of people running a business doing that remotely, rather than meeting together in the same place physically, weren't really examined at all. Of course this may not be relevant to you in the start-up period of your business. But if there is more than one person in the business, it's a very real issue. In businesses with more than one person, but where there are business premises, the practice of "hot desking" had become popular long before Covid. This was the idea that people could be in and out of the office at irregular intervals, and, rather than having a fixed place which was theirs and theirs only, they could occupy any desk which had a computer terminal on it, when they happened to be at the business HQ. Hot desking was generally popular in businesses where workers needed to be out and about for a high proportion of the time: for example accountants away working at clients' premises. But on first sight it seems obvious that this sort of technique, in conjunction with working at home, is a brilliant way of minimising the amount of permanent space you actually need. And this is what gives us some cause for concern. The benefits of working together with others in the same job and same business is something which it is very difficult to measure in pounds and pence. But we think undoubtedly it can be an important ingredient in many business' success. Of course, you can have zoom meetings and conference calls. But these are nothing like such effective means of communication as a relaxed and unscheduled (so to speak) sharing of thoughts and ideas. And remember the important fact, that comparatively well-heeled business owners often overlook, that not everyone's home is particularly easy to work in.

So our message is clear, although it may not be that easy to implement in practice: you need to arrive at a balance, when running a business involving more than one person, between the wish to save money by keeping everyone at home on the one hand, and the need for free and relaxed communication between workers, and effective use of the working day on the other hand.

Is it in the Budget?

Dragging the discussion back forcibly again from the absorbing (and very important) subject of avoiding false economy, how do you, in actual practical terms, control overheads which have a natural tendency to creep upwards if a careful eye isn't kept on them? We've warned about the counterproductive practice of spending too much valuable time on looking after the pennies, but how in practice do you avoid this trap?

One good way is to do it is to set a budget. This is a useful discipline in any event but it can provide a very useful and quick check against proliferating expenditure. When considering incurring overhead expense, the simple question "is it in the budget" is both a simple one to ask and as simple one to answer. If a given item of expense isn't in the budget, there are only two possible reasons for this: either the expenditure isn't necessary, and so should be rejected, or it is necessary and the budget was wrongly prepared. In the latter case, of course, you should go ahead and spend the money – and change the budget.

The Growth of "Admin"

Finally, a warning against a disease which afflicts almost all businesses at one time or another in their lives: the ever growing monster which is your business' admin function. By admin we mean, generally, expenditure which is so interior to the business, so to speak, that it is far removed from anything which would tend to increase the business' turnover. We have found by experience that this is a growth (to change the metaphor) that needs regular pruning to avoid it strangling the healthy and productive parts of the business, and destroying its profitability.

And here we have another paradox: a very important tool

in assessing whether the admin function is getting out of control is to have reliable and sufficiently frequent management accounts. But the internal accounting function of the business is itself an example of admin that can easily overtake the original function for which it has been set up, and become almost an end in itself. Accounts are important, of course: who are we to cast any doubt on that statement? But accounts can easily become so detailed, and frequent, as to become more a waste of time than a useful management tool. You'll soon get to establish for yourself what are the key figures you need to run the business, and a fully worked out and balanced set of management accounts, whilst it may warm the cockles of your internal accountant's heart, are often far more of a luxurious product than you actually need. The motto here is: get the key figures, even if on a "quick and dirty" basis, and forget the rest – leave it to the accountant and auditors at the year end who are producing accounts for a quite different purpose.

CHAPTER 12
COMMON MISTAKES IN BUSINESS

It may seem negative to devote a chapter to things that you can do wrong in business, but of course the point is that forewarned is forearmed, and although it's important to concentrate on the positive side, in particular how to increase the "top line" of the business, you will also need to make sure that you don't ruin the results of all your hard work by making some silly mistake.

This is above all a practical guide to starting-up and running your own business, and none of the business errors that follow are in any way academic or theoretical: they're all mistakes that we've seen clients making in the real world. So welcome to our chamber of horrors, which we list out in no particular order.

Overtrading

We'll start with a mistake that, paradoxically perhaps, results from excessive keenness and even excessive success. Overtrading is a classic mistake made by an inexperienced entrepreneur. What it basically consists in is taking on more work than the financial resources available to you enable you to fund, and it's a surprisingly easy trap to fall into. The following example comes from a real life situation.

John has decided to take the self employment "plunge", and leave his safe, but ill-paid, job with a large company as an electrical engineer. He's seen that the prices he is being charged out at by his employer to customers are a multiple of several times what he actually gets paid for his labour. So he forms Honest John Electrics Limited and puts the word out at his local working men's club that he is available for sub-contract and domestic work. At first, predictably, everything goes swimmingly. He finds that he's got quite enough work to fill the working week, indeed far too much. He's obliging and his work is good. So he takes on an assistant, and charges that assistant out at three times the actual cost of employing him. In no time (and it's the speed with which things happen that is the problem) he's found that he has enough work to take on three or four workers, and things reach the stage where it's no longer possible to run the business from his kitchen table. So he rents a small workshop, where tools and supplies are kept overnight, and vans parked.

The business is extremely profitable, and the business model almost ideal. With a series of small jobs, mostly at people's houses, but from time to time working as sub-contractors on construction sites where payment is made regularly, the cash flows in very nicely, and John starts to enjoy a significantly improved lifestyle.

Then he receives an invitation to tender for doing all the electrical fittings in a major new commercial building that is being constructed. In order to meet the tight contractual deadlines, he calculates that he will need nearly to double the size of his workforce. However, the profit which he is set to make is quite eye-watering. So takes on the extra staff, signs the contract on the dotted line, and moves almost the whole of his workforce on to the big contract. Six months later, his company is put in insolvent liquidation.

What went wrong? The problem wasn't that his principal was slow in paying his invoices. The problem is quite simply that there is inevitably an interval, even when you are paid bang on time, between your paying out for materials and wages on the one side and receiving payment on the other. In accounting terms, you have an issue in funding your work-in-progress. In John's case, as a cash-flow forecast would have predicted, the financial amount sunk in work-in-progress was greater than his resources. His overdraft at the bank spiralled out of control, and eventually the bank stopped honouring payments. As soon as suppliers caught wind of this, they put John on "stop", and he became unable to fulfil the requirements of the contract. Basically, although the big contact was massively in the black as far as profit and loss is concerned, as far as cash resources were concerned, it was just much too big for him.

The moral of the story, of course, which is based, as we say, on a real life incident, is that there are times when you just have to say "no". This is no doubt a very difficult thing indeed to do, especially when the glittering prizes of a big order are dangled in front of your eyes. But so, sometimes, it has to be.

Lack of Focus

Sometimes a business suffers because those who run it try to do too many different things, or try to do too many things at once. This is endemic in small family building firms, to take one example. Who hasn't come across the headbanging situation of a builder whom it's impossible to keep on site for long enough to finish the job? So failing to finish anything, because you're starting too many other jobs, is another classic reason for business failure. Most customers have a rooted and understandable objection to paying before the job is finished or the goods are delivered.

But lack of focus can also cause problems when it's not just a case of taking on too much work, but of taking on too many different sorts of work. The old phrase "Jack of all trades and master of none" sums up the problem here. If you don't know what you're doing, because you are unfamiliar with the product or service you're selling, you're only going to make money out of it by good luck.

Limiting your Field

Inevitably, when warning budding entrepreneurs about the dangers of spreading themselves too thinly, there's the opposite fault to take care to avoid, as well. Sometimes a business fails to grow because opportunities to grow and diversify are simply not grasped. So it's important to try and get a balance here between these two opposite errors.

If all this seems very difficult, and you're starting to despair, already, of steering the ship of your business clear of all these rocks, don't be discouraged: the very fact that you're reading this book, and thinking about the problems, places you in a league above the vast majority (we would say) of those running new or start-up businesses. All we're trying to do here is give a steer to your basic common sense, which hopefully will be sufficient to enable you to give enough thought, but not too much, to the possible problems in order to avoid them.

Too Much Reliance on One Customer

In a way, this issue could be seen as being allied with the over trading problem that we started off by describing. It doesn't take much imagination to see that total reliance on a single customer can end in tears. That customer might fail, take away their custom, or even simply strangle your business by paying you slowly. Sometimes, no doubt, a business person will have no option but to put all their eggs in one basket. There are some types of service where by definition there is only one customer, for example businesses which provide goods or services to large government and other public sector entities. But even here it may be possible to diversify your customer base, and you should certainly always be on the look out for opportunities of doing this, as the following example shows.

As part of a move to privatise the provision of public goods and services, the civil engineering department of Muggleton Borough Council has morphed into MBC CivEng Limited, a private company owned by four of the previous heads of the department. The council, as part of the deal, guarantees them at least as much work as they had whilst they were working in-house, for a minimum period of four years. And in the event this promise is more than adequately fulfilled. The staff and directors of the company are worked off their feet to keep the council happy. As such, they've neither the time nor the inclination to look around for other civil engineering clients. All except for one of the directors, Cynthia, who realises the danger that lies ahead. She spends her evenings and weekends working away at other possible contacts who might provide work, and her efforts bear fruit in the form of a substantial retainer awarded by a big multinational PLC for looking after its civil engineering needs.

The other directors are horrified when she tells them that she's got even more work for the company: but this action pays off when, after the four year period is over, the borough council suddenly decides to put out its civil engineering needs to tender, and MBC CivEng is (inevitably) squeezed out by a major firm coming down from London, which is able to treat this initial contract as a "loss leader".

No Contingency Plan

Taking a general moral from the above story, one way you could put it is that, before Cynthia took matters into her own hands, the company had no contingency plan. This principle doesn't just apply to the contingency of your single customer going elsewhere, but also applies to all kinds of other things that can go wrong in business: a fire or other natural disaster, legislation which makes it impossible to carry on trading in the way you have done, a falling off in demand for your product due to economic or other factors, and so on and so on. In our chapter about business plans, we made the point that your plan will look much more impressive to third party readers if it has a clear contingency plan built into it. Obviously the importance of having such a contingency plan isn't just for the purpose of impressing potential investors, though: it's also important to preserve the very existence of your business if things actually do go disastrously wrong.

Too Much Reliance on a Single Product

We may be wronging the company, because we aren't au fait with the inner workings of history, but what does the word Kodak immediately bring to mind? For most people it's going to be a completely obsolete product, which is camera film. Similarly, we don't know what big oil companies are going to do when oil either runs out or the burning of it is basically legislated out of existence. We expect that the big oil companies are well aware of this issue, and will have been working on a new type of product, or basic use of their product, for many years now. But what applies to the big multinational companies, in this instance, applies even more to the small and start up business.

Again, it's a case of having a contingency plan if your single product is likely to fall out of favour. This obviously won't apply to some types of business: unless they come up with a self-cleaning window, for example.

Limiting Resources

If we had to name one single mistake which was responsible for the most harm caused to young businesses, it would be the fault of "stinginess" or limiting the resources of available to the business. We've said something about this is in our chapter about controlling overheads, and the important point we were trying to make there is that not all "overhead" costs are actually just "dead" costs. All kinds of expenditure, not just what accountants sometimes refer to as the direct "costs of sale", can have the effect of enabling you to expand the turnover of the business.

The problem with excessive limitation of resources is that those responsible for doing it, who are running the business, may be only dimly aware of the damage their approach is causing. Just one order that you have to turn away, or fail to deliver on time, can have an exponential effect on the inclination of would be customers to come back to you. You are strangling expansion which could have made you rich.

Our definite impression is that this problem afflicts not just some, but the vast majority of businesses. The businesses that you see expanding rapidly, and proceeding through all the stages of small family business, to large family business, to quoted business, are ones where the brake has been taken off expansion by a proper resourcing of what the business does.

To us, this is a good illustration of how success in business is very rarely a conceptually complex thing: more often it's the failure to see simple things which holds a business back.

Not Keeping Up-to-date Figures

This can be a very serious error indeed, and it is etched on our memory after a client which, at that time, was our largest client of all, went ignominiously bust mainly because of this neglect of basic management accounting. The following is a fictionalised version of what happened in this real life business disaster.

At one time Major Slip-up and his wife Dorothy were the envy of their neighbours and, indeed, the local business community. On his retirement from the army, Major Slip-up bought a large house which he converted into a care home. This did well, in the days before red tape had strangled the residential care industry to quite the extent it has since; and Major and Mrs Slip-up soon found themselves expanding into a group of three care homes. They were helped in this by a really good bookkeeper, who provided regular management figures showing, for example, which of the homes were more profitable than others, and why. In fact, that she was more than a bookkeeper, properly speaking: she was more like a finance director in the actual value and importance of her input to the running of the business. Things went well, and Major and Mrs Slip-up started regarding the care home group as effectively no more than a cash cow to fund their reasonably lavish lifestyle. Then an incident which didn't seem important at the time, but was actually the death knell for the whole business, occurred: the bookkeeper left on maternity leave, and decided not to come back. Major and Mrs Slip-up took on a new bookkeeper, a middle aged man who had had a number of jobs in quick succession with high street firms of accountants. All of a sudden, in place of the timely and regular management figures (which, to be honest, Major Slip-up had fallen into the habit of scanning only briefly) the flow of information suddenly came to a halt. The bookkeeper always had some reason for the figures being in a mess, and not being produced at all, let alone on time. Things went on like this for a matter of years, and Major and Mrs Slip-up found that, mysteriously, despite the homes all being still pretty much full, the bank overdraft of the company was galloping out of control. The bank, which had an unlimited personal guarantee signed by Major Slip-up, and secured on their house when things were good, seemed fairly relaxed about this, at least for a time.

Then things changed for the company on the accountancy front. AAA Aardvark Tax Advisers LLP were appointed, not so much because the clients were unhappy about their accounting situation (although they were) but because somebody had told them that AAA Aardvark could save them lots of corporation tax. The first thing that the senior partner of this new firm said was "we need to get reliable figures for the last three years, before we can even think about tax planning." So the accounting staff of the new firm got to work on the chaotic records of the company, and after great difficulty hammered together draft accounts for the previous three years (which had been outstanding despite increasingly threatening messages from Companies House).

These figures revealed that the staff to fee ratio of the care homes was way higher than the industry standard and, indeed, way above the point in which the business was viable. By not looking at the figures, Major and Mrs Slip-up had simply been blissfully unaware of the fact that they were paying their staff far too much for the income the homes were bringing in.

Tax turned out to be the last of the company's problems. It was wound up insolvent not very long after this, and Major and Mrs Slip-up had to sell their house. All because they didn't keep up to date management accounting figures.

Not Allowing for Tax

In some ways, our tax system could be accused of being an invitation to business people to be other than frugal, especially in the early periods of the business. A business which starts on say 6 April 2021, and makes its first accounts to 5 April 2022, may not have to pay any tax until 31 January 2023: nearly two years, perhaps, after profits have started rolling in. For limited companies, the timing is that tax is paid nine months after the end of the accounting period. This is fine if your profits are steady, or on an upward trajectory, but sometimes it can happen that a tax bill crops up when business is not looking so good, and cash flow is perhaps, very difficult. Woe to the entrepreneur who has not kept money aside to pay the tax! Although we have to say that, generally speaking, we have a friendlyish tax collecting body in the UK, their patience can be exhausted; and a time comes when tax arrears could seriously threaten the future of the business; quite apart from absorbing an undue amount of the entrepreneur's time and anxiety.

This problem, of tax liabilities which haven't been anticipated coming home to roost, can be particularly acute where the business is run through a limited company. The point about the limited company as a business structure, as we commented in an earlier chapter, is that the company's money is the company's, and your money is yours: and it is a wise man who knows the difference. Quite often, the main entrepreneur in the business is far from wise in this respect, and effectively treats the company's bank account as an extension to his own. Very often indeed, in practice, we find, when we come to do the year end accounts for such a company, that the main director/shareholder has taken all of the company's profits out for personal expenditure. The problem with this is that it gives rise to a substantial personal tax charge, which may be in addition to the tax charge that the company is paying on its profits. And to make things far worse, the tax charge is arrived at by a process, effectively, of "grossing up" the amount taken out of the company by the individual. So, if an individual has, say, taken £100,000 out in cash over the course of the year, this is likely to be treated, if formalised as remuneration, as a gross figure of something like £160,000, on which £60,000 tax and employee's national insurance, and perhaps another £20,000 employer's national insurance, is due. And in a typical case of this sort, the company has little or no money to pay this – nor has the individual, because, typically, he will have spent the money by this point.

So, if you don't want to give yourself a huge tax headache, eschew completely the "live now, pay later" approach to dealing with your business' money.

Not Keeping Debtors Under Control

Finally, a very straightforward error, but one which a high proportion of businesses fall into. Unless yours is the sort of business which operates purely on a cash basis, that is, you are paid cash at the same time as, or before, you provide your goods or services, the issue of giving credit, and allowing customers/clients to abuse your trust, is one that you neglect at your peril. It's very easy, though, as we know from personal experience, to let your credit control slip, whilst you concentrate your efforts on the much more interesting job of bringing in new work. But if you look at how much some people owe you, you can be astonished, if you fail to keep a regular grip on it over the preceding period. The real problem is that basically most of us are nice people, and are too well mannered to thump our fists (metaphorically speaking) on our client's and customer's desks and demand money. In this way, those in business who aren't quite so nice get away with funding their own businesses or lifestyles by way of what is effectively an interest free loan from you. Sometimes it isn't malice aforethought, of course. It's simply that some people forget to pay, or defer paying, if no pressure is applied to them: the inertia principle. And sometimes they simply can't pay, because they are in financial difficulties. But if this is the case, you should stop supplying them straight away, unless you want to set up as a charity rather than a commercial business.

CHAPTER 13
WHAT IF THINGS GO WRONG? ASSET PROTECTION MADE SIMPLE

It's appropriate, if you're superstitious, that Chapter 13 of our guide to setting up in business is all about the possibility of things going horribly wrong, and how to guard against this possibility. Nothing in life is 100% safe, and anyone who thinks it is, or could be made so, frankly shouldn't be going into business. Things can and do go wrong in the real world, and the wise person is somebody who takes that possibility into account and takes all reasonable precautions against it. You'll find out, by reading this chapter, what those precautions are.

The average reader of Victorian novels, by people like Dickens and his friend Mrs Gaskell, is apt to get a fairly one sided view of what business is about: the point of view of the long suffering workers. The mill owner is portrayed living in his fancy house outside the area polluted by the smoke of his factory chimneys with his la-di-da young daughters carefully shielded from the harsh realities of life a handful of miles away. The gaffer's got so much money, is the message you get from these novels, that it wouldn't hurt him to pay an extra penny an hour to his poor wage slaves huddled together in insanitary inner city conditions. What the novelist doesn't say (because the novelist isn't, generally, a business person) is that to run any kind of business enterprise is to be on a constant knife edge between success and failure. Obviously it's all too easy to over simplify, and that's a danger on both the left and the right hand sides of the political spectrum, but a fundamental problem that business grapples with is that those who do take the risks, and put in all the extra time and anxiety into running a business, are a tiny minority numerically speaking. Hence the lack of general public interest in the harsh realities faced by business owners. Paying his employees that extra penny an hour could indeed have made the difference between success and failure for the Victorian mill owner.

What all this near political commentary is working towards, apart from the fact that making a success in business isn't by any means a picnic, is that taking all possible precautions that the law allows to protect yourself in the event of financial disaster is in no way to be blamed by those not taking similar risks. The existence of a thriving business community is essential to the wellbeing of any country, because, ultimately, it's business that pays not just some of the tax, but all of the tax which keeps the state finances going. Make it too difficult for entrepreneurs to protect themselves and their assets from external attack, and you end up stifling enterprise altogether: and everybody suffers.

All that by way of general comment. But it's true to say that different sorts of business have different levels of risk. Being professionals ourselves, we would probably put the professions, and in particular some of them, at the top end of the risk spectrum. A person providing professional services is paid for his expertise, and is paid specifically to get things right. Any mistakes are invariably labelled by the lawyers as "negligence", with potentially catastrophic results. But it's also true to say that the provision of goods or services generally which are high volume and low margin, is high risk sort of business. A low margin can so easily veer off into no margin, and if your business depends on turning over a high figure, small percentage changes can make the difference between profit and loss.

So we would start off by suggesting to our target readership, those who are starting up in business, that they seriously consider the level of financial risk that their particular business proposition brings with it. Although there is some correlation between risk and reward, it isn't a direct one. Is there another sort of business you are fitted to carry out that doesn't bring with it that kind of risk? Are there risky elements of your business which are not essential to the whole thing, and which could be avoided? Should you set strict financial limits to certain parts of the business, that you make sure you don't stray beyond? If you don't address this sort of fundamental question at the planning stage, it's likely that you won't have the time or attention to do so once the business is fully up and running,

Insuring Against Risk

Some types of insurance are compulsory (like motor insurance and employer's liability), but there are others where the business basically has the choice as to whether to insure. We recommend talking to an insurance broker at the outset of business to find out what types of insurance are available, and precisely what risks they guard against – and don't guard against. But the important point we need to make here is that insurance isn't, and can never be, a complete answer to protecting yourself from business risk. For a start, there are many kinds of financial attack that you simply can't insure against. Examples of this are tax investigations which end up with large unprovided liabilities (which, in the real world, we can assure you, can happen even if you're innocent of any tax irregularity); downturns in the economy which affect your business and make it no longer viable; and changes in government legislation that have a similar effect.

And you should also remember that insurance is like a suit of armour which has chinks and weak places in it. Most insurance companies will do their best to refuse claims if they can possibly find the small print to justify it: or if there were any mistakes, deliberate or otherwise, in your application form. So don't regard an insurance policy as an infallible protection.

The Three Types of Financial Risk: And Ways of Guarding Against Them

There are three sorts of unpleasant financial outcome from things going wrong in a business:

- You can lose the money you've invested in the business; or
- The business can go bust and you can lose assets employed in the business (like properties); or
- You can end up with liabilities that attach to you personally, as an individual, and affect your non business assets.

The first of these, losing the money you've invested, whilst painful, is probably the least so of the three sorts of financial disaster we're talking about. Any business set-up is a risky investment, where you hope to make a very good return indeed – much better you could get by investing the money in the bank or say quoted shares – but brings with it corre-sponding risk of loss. That's the way the world works. But can you protect yourself in any way against the loss of your investment?

We can think of one way, and it's one which is surprisingly little used in practice. When a business goes under, for example a business run as a limited company, it's normally the case that creditors of the business end up not getting paid. And very often one of the creditors is the business owner him or herself. Perhaps they may have put money into the business by way of loan, or share capital, and got nothing back in return. But it's possible, if you're the business owner, to take out a charge on the company's assets, in the same way a bank does when it lends money to a company. This legal charge, which can be against fixed assets of the business like premises or plant or vehicles, or a floating charge against the working capital of the business, mean that you, as the business owner, would take priority in the event of a winding up over or other creditors, basically, except for somebody who has a charge that takes precedence over yours. (The bank will always fall into this category if it is lending secured.)

Protecting the Business Assets

You might think, in the event of an insolvent winding up of your trading business, that it's inevitable that you would lose all of the assets utilised in the business, for example, buildings, plant, vehicles, and things like trademarks, patents, and the business "goodwill". This need not be the case! Have a read of the example that follows, which illustrates a situation where the business is able easily to rise from the ashes of its financial ruin:

Jeff Boozer leaves his well paid job as head brewer of the beer division of a large chemicals conglomerate in the Midlands, and, using his savings and an inheritance from his grandfather, he sets up his own pub with attached microbrewery. Acting on advice from his accountant, he buys the building, and brewing equipment, in a holding company, Boozer Holdings Limited. He soon builds up a very good reputation for his Under the Table pale ale, and "Driller Killer" strong bitter. These names become so popular, up and down the country, in fact, that he registers them as trademarks in the name of Boozer Holdings Limited. The actual brewing, and operation of the pub, though, are run by two 100% owned subsidiaries, Stitch in Time Limited, and Boozer's Brewery Limited. Things go swimmingly well until, after 5 years, of very successful trading, a visit from HMRC uncovers a systemic error in the calculation of beer duty. A massive bill for back duty, interest, and penalties is duly served on Boozer's Brewery Limited, which pushes it well over the wrong side of the insolvency line. The brewery company duly calls in the liquidators, and expires, lamented by all.

*Fortunately, though, Jeff has made sure that, amongst the few assets of Boozer's Brewery Limited is **not** numbered any amount owed to it by the holding company. So, whilst the trading subsidiary goes bust, the holding company is untouched by the disaster, and Jeff retains control over the building, equipment, and trademarks, enabling him to set up a phoenix company which hopefully won't make the same tax error again.*

In our example, the holding company and trading subsidiary structure was set up at the outset, and of course the key to the situation is that the holding company doesn't carry out any trading activity itself, but merely owns the asset. Hence it's very unlikely to incur any kind of liability which would put those assets at risk. For businesses which haven't been set up in this way from day one, the good news is that it's quite easy to move from, say, a situation where a company both trades and owns the valuable assets, and a situation where the valuable assets have been moved up into a non trading holding company. There are two ways of doing this:

- The company continues to own the assets, but forms a 100% subsidiary into which it "hives down" the trading activities; or
- A newly formed holding company issues shares to the current shareholders of the trading company in exchange for their shareholdings, so that the trading company becomes a 100% subsidiary. The valuable assets, such as buildings, plant and intangible assets are then "hived up" to the new holding company.

Although the second way of doing things is more of a palaver, involving, amongst a lot of other formalities, application for HMRC clearance, it has the advantage that the new holding company has no history of trading, and therefore if any problems come out of the woodwork in the future from the trading period, the holding company is unaffected by it. This might not necessarily be the case with the first, or "hive down" route, where a problem might arise that dates back to the period before the hive down, and therefore puts the assets that the company still owns at risk.

Limited Liability

And then we come to the third and last type of financial disaster, which threatens not just the investment in the business, and the business assets themselves, but also the personal assets of the business owners.

In our chapter about choosing the right business structure, we mentioned four types of business vehicles which are in common use: the sole tradership, the partnership, the limited company and the Limited Liability Partnership (LLP). Of these the first two structures bring with them unlimited liability: so if the business goes bust, the sole trader's or partners' personal assets are on the line, assuming that the assets of the business are insufficient to pay creditors. Limited companies, and their young cousins LLP's, provide protection against this, because the liabilities, in the event of insolvency, basically stick with the business entity, so that if they are wound up insolvent it is the creditors that lose out rather than the business owners. As to the choice between using a limited company and using an LLP, in practice this is likely to be dictated by tax considerations, and you should refer to our chapter on the business structure for the key considerations in choosing between these. But there's a different class of liabilities against which even limited companies and LLP's don't protect you, and this last, most difficult category of liabilities is what we come on to consider next.

Personal Liabilities

Limited companies and LLP's provide a lot of protection, but they don't protect you, for example, against liabilities that you have personally guaranteed, such as loans from banks, and rental payments to landlords. Also, they don't protect you against certain types of legal action where you yourself are at fault (as opposed to one of your employees, say): claims in negligence, defamation (a problem for publishers), or various types of wrong doing which enable authorities to "lift the corporate veil". How can you protect yourself against these?

Well, it may seem obvious, but the first thing is to avoid giving personal guarantees if at all possible. Sometimes it is possible, for example, to get bank lending secured solely on the business assets rather than backed up by personal guarantees, by "shopping around" amongst the various banks. A firm refusal to give a PG will also sometimes influence landlords who ask for their rents to be so guaranteed: if they think that you will simply go elsewhere, to other premises, if they insist.

And the only advice we can come up with, as regards personal claims for things like negligence, is to avoid to whatever extent possible the kind of situation, and indeed even the kind of business, where such claims are a serious risk.

Asset Protection

But once you've said that, you're still left with an irreducible minimum risk of personal liability: either because we're human and can't help doing things wrong, or because your only skill, and ability to make money, lies in a field where negligence claims are possible. Hence there comes about a whole industry which has existed in the United States for many years, aimed at asset protection. In the UK, we're nowhere near so far along the line, and the following suggestions are inevitably made tentatively, because of the fact that the law is developing still in the whole area of asset protection.

One method of asset protection that is apparently popular on the other side of the Atlantic is setting up trusts. By putting your assets in trust for yourself and members of your family, you are putting them outside your own personal ownership and control, at least in theory. So, the theory goes, if you were ever to be made bankrupt by a disastrous personal claim, the assets put in trust are safe, and can still be used for your personal benefit at the trustees' discretion.

We don't know how these work in the US but in the United Kingdom there is a big tax difficulty about simply putting everything you've got on trust. This is that there is a charge to inheritance tax at 20% to the extent that you put more than the nil rate band for that tax (currently £325,000) into a trust over a cumulative period of seven years. So trusts are only practicable, in this situation, for small amounts and for "business assets", which qualify for 100% inheritance tax relief.

As an alternative to putting assets on trust, you can give them to your spouse or life partner. Again there's a problem with gifts to a person other than a spouse, and this time it's capital gains tax rather than inheritance tax. A gift is treated, for CGT purposes, as if it were a sale of the assets concerned for their market value. The exception to this is gifts between spouses and civil partners, which are treated as CGT neutral effectively.

The big imponderable with both of these methods of asset protection involving transferring the ownership to someone else is that the law in this country has safeguards in place to avoid creditors being left out in the cold by such actions. If the asset transfer takes place either too soon before a person's insolvency, or can be shown to have been done specifically to avoid paying given creditors, then our understanding (as non insolvency specialists) is that the transfers can be reversed. So it's better to do this sort of thing sooner rather than later, and ideally before you have an inkling that there is in fact a specific financial problem on the horizon.

Cheer Up: It May Never Happen!

Inevitably reading a chapter like this, which solves a lot of your potential future financial problems but not all of them, has a tendency to have a rather depressing effect. But it's always worth remembering that the risk which carrying on a business brings with it is only the flip side to the huge potential rewards. As we started off this book by saying, almost nobody gets to live in one of those beautiful mansions in "millionaire's row" or in the country by working for someone else, and everyone who has got there has done so by taking calculated risks. And if you actually look at the number of people who end up ruined and destitute, selling matchboxes on the street, it's a tiny minority that suffer disaster. In reality there is usually life afterwards: often, rightly or wrongly, with no apparent reduction in the quality of the person's lifestyle.

CHAPTER 14

WORKING IN THE BUSINESS AND WORKING ON THE BUSINESS

The difference between working in the business and working on the business is an absolutely crucial one to understand. No doubt when you're in the business start-up stage your time will be largely taken up with the first sort of work: making things happen, organising, doing basically almost everything. You haven't got the luxury of taking a step back and thinking a bit about how you do things, and indeed why you do some things. But a time will come, and the sooner it comes the better, when you're no longer so busy that you can't see the wood for the trees.

So, to be clear, working in the business is doing all the same old tasks day after day and week after week, which carrying on the business consists in: making sales, dealing with problems, planning the day, week or months ahead. Working on the business, on the other hand, could be seen as a luxury. In means stopping, for a predetermined amount of time, and looking at the way the business runs, as it were from outside. Asking those questions that you normally don't have the time to ask. Giving your mind the space to think laterally about what you're basically trying to achieve, and different possible ways of achieving it. Preferably talking things through with somebody who is intelligent enough, even if he or she doesn't know much about your particular business, to make comments and even suggestions that work as a kind of catalyst for your own creative juices.

So we're setting out, as a basic framework for the working on the business process, a number of suggestions in this chapter for areas which may repay leisured thought; and hopefully this can be used as a basic framework for a general review of the business, on a periodic basis. Make no mistake about it, though: if you don't force yourself to make time for this potentially very valuable exercise to take place, your "default" position is going to be working in the business, and possibly working harder and less efficiently than you could otherwise be doing. In our experience as advisers to business people, we've far more often seen the phenomenon of the enterprise which is well and truly stuck in a groove, than we've seen instances of business people who feel able to leave the shop to mind itself for a time and apply some basic common sense (brilliant intelligence is very rarely needed) to the problem of how to make things run more smoothly and profitably.

As we've had to say many times in this book, any framework or set of ideas which is designed to be useful for almost any kind of business is going to contain a lot of items which are simply of no relevance in your particular circumstances. So, if you like to regard what follows as a kind of checklist, the words "not applicable" are inevitably going to be written against some of them. But we don't think that takes anything away from the usefulness of the framework taken as a whole.

1. Efficiency

Efficiency is a very vague and generalised term, but there is not a single business on this earth which doesn't need it, and in which the general level of efficiency couldn't be improved in one way or another. One possible definition of efficiency is having systems and making sure that they actually operate. The two aren't necessarily the same thing. An efficient system is one which needs the least number of stages possible in order to take a process from A to Z. So one of the least efficient arrangements you can have, for example, is one where a number of different people need to approve, initial, rubberstamp, or whatever anything which is done or any document which is produced. Inevitably where you have a chain of people like this, someone is going to be away, or not at their desk at that particular moment, and the whole process gets held up. The art of devising an efficient system is to make as few such stages as possible, whilst balancing the need to be doing things to a sufficiently high standard.

One way to improve efficiency is to have a set time in each day, or a set day in each week, which you invariably give to a particular important task. This can involve quite a bit of discipline. It's so easy just to go at whatever is right in front of your nose, and postpone dealing with things which are equally important, or perhaps more important, but have got submerged beneath a pile of other tasks (either metaphorically or literally). For example, a certain type of business might set aside the time from 9:00 to 10:00 each morning to dealing with post, from 10:00 till 10:30 planning the rest of the day's work; and so on.

Avoid staff meetings if you possibly can, because these are the biggest thieves of time, and the biggest generators of inefficiency, that is known to any business. Certainly avoid having meetings just for the sake of having meetings. If there is some really important issue that comes up, that can only be dealt with by interactive, face-to-face discussion, then call a meeting to discuss just that point. Avoid the endless waste of time generated by the "any other business" syndrome. If you find you have to have staff meetings, make sure you have

someone in the chair whose aim is to get the business trans-
acted as quickly as it reasonably can.

But what, you might say, about the sort of meeting which
is set up for the purpose of working "on the business"? A
ruthless chairman, and a strong emphasis on dealing with a
specific point and that point only, surely destroys any hope of
anyone arriving at the kind of "lightbulb moments" and
lateral thinking that we've just been praising as being good
for a business?

Quite frankly, we have severe reservations about the use
of "brainstorming" sessions, "away days" and so on, where a
number of people meet together to talk about nothing in
particular. We've experienced these ourselves, in our previous
firms, and we can quite confidently say that none of the ideas
that have ever been come up in such a meeting have been
usefully implemented afterwards. The cynical view is that
these events are just organised by one or two people who
want to get away from their spouses and have an opportunity
for a drink and a relax, away from the urgent requirements of
work.

No, the sort of working "on" the business that we're advocating here is not a kind of loosely constituted committee, but,
normally, an individual, or at most two individuals, concentrating hard on the task at hand and coming up with a plan
which is actually going to be implemented. Our attitude to
committees, and their general suitability for purpose, is best
summed up by the joker who described a camel as a "horse
designed by a committee". So hold fewer or, if at all possible,
no meetings!

Another important element in efficiency is how you
communicate. What we are about to say shouldn't need
saying, but unfortunately in the realities of today's world, it
definitely does. Which one of us hasn't felt the strong tempta-
tion to communicate with someone else by email or text when
it is much quicker to pick up the phone, or, if they're within

reach, go and speak to them face-to-face? Email is an incredibly inefficient form of communication. You receive an email from a colleague asking a question at 9.07 in the morning, you put this to one side, because there are a lot of things to get off your desk first, and then you go out to do some work. Later on in the day you realise that you haven't answered the email yet, and, after two interruptions which result in drafting the email taking nearly an hour, you send off the answer. This arrives too late for the person who asked the question to read it, and so therefore he comes back to you sometime the next day with further questions that your answer has given rise to. And so on. This scenario is all too plausible and realistic in our experience, and often the thing could be dealt with by way of a ten minute telephone conversation which might save several days in practice as compared with email. So one of the fruits of your session working on the business might be to set up a protocol (even if it's only for your own use) as to how different types of message will be communicated.

2. Setting a Budget

Budgets aren't necessary or useful in all businesses, but in some they're an invaluable way of making you look hard at the financial incomings and outgoings, which are the lifeblood of a business. Ultimately anything you do in the course of running your business matters solely to the extent that it either increases your income or reduces your outgoings. So the exercise and discipline of setting a budget concentrates the mind on or the most essential aspects of the business. Setting a budget is one of the most important ways you can work on the business. Some sorts of business respond better than others to this, though. In the sort of business where your income is genuinely completely unpredictable, the likelihood is that your expenses will be unpredictable too. Don't waste your time with excel spreadsheets if you're in this sort of business. Getting back to the subject of efficiency, though, if the business is that very common sort which would benefit from a budgeting process, make sure that (a) you set the budget on a timely and regular basis (normally once a year, just before the year begins); and (b) make sure that you go through checking actual expenditure and income against budget. An obvious point perhaps, but one which it is too often neglected.

3. New Products

On the one hand, it's true to say that "if it works, don't fix it". On the other, the possibility of there being new types of goods or services that you could sell, that you're not selling at the moment, mustn't be discounted. This is par excellence the sort of thing which you're never going to have the time to think out if you spend all of your time working in the business. It may not be an entirely new "product", but may be new, more efficient ways of producing something similar to what you do now. Pardon the very vague and general wording here, but this is a book for all types of business.

4. Sorting the Sheep from the Goats

Almost any business which is other than completely monolithic will have good parts and bad parts. Take a step back from your business, then, and take a long cool look at which parts are good and which parts are bad. Again, this is the sort of thing that's obvious: but only when you think about it. And you only think about it when you take time off from doing it. The result is that we've seen countless businesses wasting their substance, and devoting their resources, to flogging a number of dead horses, whilst the one live horse is left idly chewing the grass at one side. And when you point this out, the feeling of relief with which they realise that they don't have to carry on working so hard for no or little return any more, makes the whole exercise more than worthwhile.

All this seems very simple: carry on with the profitable parts of the business and jettison the unprofitable. But this simple advice needs to come with two very important health warnings.

Firstly, where you have a number of business lines in a single entity, make sure that you're correctly unravelling the actual costs that genuinely apply to each division. A very slight alteration in the principle of how you allocate costs can make a part of the business which is actually contributing to the whole look as though it's loss making. Avoid over simplistic accountancy.

Secondly, don't kill off a product, service, or division simply because it's loss making, if relatively straightforward "tweaking" could make it profitable. It's hard work creating a new line of business, or a new product. Don't waste the hard work that you've already put in if you don't need to.

5. Staffing

Very often the only real problem with a business is the lack of adequate staffing, because the hardest thing about running many businesses is deciding what sort of level of staff you require. On the one hand, with not enough staff everyone will be busy, frazzled, and liable to make mistakes – to say nothing of stifling the expansion of the business. Too many staff, on the other hand, and the celebrated Parkinson's Law comes into effect: that work expands to fill the time allocated to it. But staffing levels can only be got right, or as near to right as is humanly possible, if you take the time and the trouble to think it through properly, according to whatever lights you've got. Don't worry about the fact that this is the kind of question that's impossible to answer correctly. If you put any thought into this as an abstract question at all, you're doing better than most businesses.

6. SWOT Analysis

This is another bit of theorising that should be taken with a pinch of salt: particularly, in the small business and business start-up context. The letters stand for "Strengths, Weaknesses, Opportunities and Threats". The idea is that you do a sort of mini health check on your business and the environment it operates in, and the aim presumably is to play to your strengths, do something about your weaknesses, seize your opportunities, and take safeguarding action against your threats. Very often, though, we've found that in practice it's just a lot of hot air, and an excuse for "consultants" (of which more below) to charge you money for telling you what you already knew.

And yet … despite its use as a piece of unthinking jargon, making it sound as though the person using these initials knows what they're talking about, the basic idea is sound: if you're not already thinking about these things anyway. In some cases (with the emphasis on the word some) doing a SWOT analysis can serve as a useful discipline, as an aid to taking your nose up from the grindstone and planning ahead a little.

7. The Customer's Eye View

This, by contrast, is one of the most revealing exercises you can go through in working on your business. Almost no one thinks seriously about how the way their business interacts with the source of its income – the clients or customers – might affect the success of the business.

You could start by logging on to your own website. In nine cases out of ten, you'll find something annoying, obscure, or difficult about using the site, which you notice quickly enough on other people's websites, but never think of considering on your own.

More generally, there's the whole experience of a customer or prospective customer in dealing with your business. If a customer calls or emails, how quickly is that customer dealt with; and how helpful and friendly is the contact?

Even more vaguely, what general impression does the business give to the outside world? Does it look scruffy, chaotic, down at heel; or efficient, friendly, and approachable?

Yet again a warning needs to be sounded here against advice which is all very well with certain types of business, but is pretty irrelevant to others. The comments about the website above are a case in point. In some businesses, particularly those selling goods on the internet, the quality, efficiency, and general user friendliness of the website is absolutely crucial and central. In other businesses, the website is little more than a glorified yellow pages entry, whose purpose is just to establish that you have some kind of existence, and to let the person who wants to contact you have the necessary details. Don't spend a lot of time on the website if you are in this category, because there are a lot better things you could be doing.

Some organisations, mostly the larger ones, take this customer eye view to much greater lengths, sending along "mystery shoppers" who are actually working under cover for the business itself, but who look, to the underlings who deal with them, as though they are genuine prospective customers. That's probably going too far for most of the entrepreneurs who are our target audience for this book: but it could be an interesting exercise in some instances.

8. Accounting Information

What we're talking about here is not so much the regular review of the historical financial information: although that's important. One of the best uses of your time when working on the business is considering exactly how much – or how little – information you actually need to run the business properly, and what format that information should be in. You might find that the current arrangements, with fully balanced quarterly management figures, for example, are far more than you need, and also take far too long to appear to be of optimum use on this.

If you sit down and think about it, you might come to the conclusion that all you need, perhaps on a weekly basis, is bank balance, the debtors and work in progress (or whatever), and the wages figure. Fully balanced and detailed profit and loss accounts may be more than you will actually read, and certainly are at a stage removed from the close handle on the controls of the business that these few key figures would give you.

Finally, traditionally a favourite device of working on the business is to appoint external consultants of some kind in order to look into the way the business works, and report with their findings and recommendations. This might be a brilliant idea in theory, although not suited to the business start-up stage very frequently; but in practice we have to say we're extremely cynical about the merit of employing external consultants. In your really big outfit, the suspicion has often been voiced that the use of consultants is simply a method of back covering for the directors. "What do you mean we haven't been running the business properly? Look at these expensive consultants we've been employing!" In the context of the smaller enterprise, our general feelings are just as cynical, but different. As we've commented before in the chapter on advisers, when we've had experience of the use of such consultants with the sort of clients we tend to advise (the smaller, owner managed sort) we've found that the process appears to consist largely of you telling the consultants all about your business, and them reading your own words back to you in an expensive and glossy report. We're probably going beyond our remit, which is to help those starting up in business, in any event, in talking about the use of external consultants. But if you are tempted by a plausible sounding salesman to engage with a marketing consultant, "business coach", or similar, think hard about it before signing on the dotted line.

CHAPTER 15
WHERE TO FIND MORE HELP

If you're one of those people who read a book from cover to cover, and you've reached this, the last section, then firstly, congratulations, and we hope you've found plenty that's useful in the preceding pages. If this were a learned treatise on the art of setting up a business, the traditional thing to do at this point would be for us to provide a list of recommended further reading. But this isn't a learned treatise, and it's not aimed at academics. Instead, as we said right at the outset, it's a practical guide to what you need to do in the real world, written by two business people based on their everyday experience of both running their own business and advising others "at the coalface".

Our intention has been to cover, in the course of this book, all the important areas and issues that someone setting up a new business will face. If any reader, indeed, feels that there are major problems with business start-up that aren't covered here, or aren't covered adequately, we would welcome your feedback, and will take it into account in preparing future editions.

But inevitably a book can't always tell you everything you need to know. It can't have look at your business and find out what the issues are, and it can't answer questions. So there may be some cases where our advice here needs to be supplemented from elsewhere.

Most people's first port of call these days is the internet. Indeed, for an awful lot of people, it's a knee jerk reaction. But if there's one message we want to get across loud and clear in this last section of our book it's this: **Don't** take anything on the world wide web as gospel. The internet shares with a book the drawback of being a passive corpus of words and pictures which knows nothing about your particular circumstances, and we don't know if you've found the same as us, that searching for answers to questions on the internet can be a very frustrating experience. How often have you found, as we have, that the passage you light on has almost, but not quite, addressed the actual issue or question you have got? And it's not always clear what authority or qualifications the writer has for providing the information.

So if a thing's worth doing, it worth doing properly. If you can't get the answer to a question in this book, consult a real person, not a computer.

As a business start-up, you may find the **Federation of Small Businesses** a useful resource. This organisation offers members financial advice, support, and the much more indirect benefit of political lobbying muscle. Member benefits include free legal advice (within limits), advice on "Crisis Management", advice and insurance against cyber-attacks, assistance with collecting money from recalcitrant debtors, and various types of insurance including insurance against HMRC investigations; together with the benefit of being able to talk to other members and pool experiences.

Then you could consider contacting, and joining, a local and/or national **Trade Association**. This is likely to be able to offer more specific and targeted advice aimed at the sort of problems and issues that arise in your own particular trade.

So far, we've been talking about free or low cost (in return for a subscription) advice. But what about the sort of advisers you pay?

Here we make an important distinction between advice on highly specific and technical problems on the one hand, and the provision of more vague and woolly "business advice" on the other. If you've read Chapter 9, you'll have seen our warning against certain types of advisers who claim to be able to increase your business profits, improve your marketing, and similar non technical services whose benefit, if there is any benefit to them, is difficult to measure. Most of these can be flushed out by the simple question: "If they're so good at running a widget factory, or cleaning the windows on office blocks, or printing glossy books for clients, why aren't they running any of these businesses themselves?" A successful and profitable business is not only much more lucrative, but also much less hard work, than setting yourself up as an expert in everybody else's businesses. So let's leave that sort of advice on one side, and look at the help that's out there, that costs you money, but actually fulfils a specific and concrete need.

For a wide range of business questions, your **accountant** is the natural first port of call. The accountant should be able to advise you on complying with your tax and VAT obligations, PAYE, record keeping, and a host of other financially based issues. Of course, some people don't appoint an accountant at all, but decide that they can go it alone. In our experience, approximately 50% of the people who decide this make the right decision. Perhaps we're unduly influenced by our experience of sorting out the mess that such people all too often get themselves into; but our advice is definitely that, if you don't know what you're doing to any extent, you should instruct an accountant to advise you: preferably at an early stage in the business start-up process.

The accountant will also be able to steer you pretty accurately, in most cases, on straightforward issues of tax planning: such as whether to operate as a limited company or not, and how to take your income from the business. But for the more complex tax questions (and, in the case of some accountants, even the simpler ones) where the accountant looks blank when you ask him a question, you will need to talk to a proper **tax adviser**. Don't make the common mistake of thinking that an accountant and a tax adviser is the same thing. Have a look at Chapter 9, again, for more discussion of this very important distinction.

So there you have it. And many readers may be tempted to ask, in surprise, "Is that all? With all the noise we hear about how important business is to the economy, and all those offering their services to help business? A short handbook, your accountant, your trade association, and possibly the FSB? What about all the courses that are out there, ranging from brief webinars to full blown MBA (Master of Business Administration) degrees?"

Well, yes. First of all, remember we're talking about start-up businesses here, where your resources both of money, and in particular, of time, are likely to be limited, and it simply isn't sensible, in our view, to devote these resources to "book learning", and information that might turn out to be useful.

In a way, this is a positive thing. How many of the great business people of the past have relied to a major extent on advice given to them by other people? We think you'll find, at the end of the day, that business success is founded, more often, not on theoretical knowledge or external advice but on the intellectual freedom (call it impatience if you like) of entrepreneurs who like to work things out for themselves – even if it means making mistakes for themselves.

So the hundred or so pages of this book may be literally all you need to get yourself started, and make sure you don't fall into any obvious traps. Also to give you a push in the right direction if you're standing, bewildered, at a crossroads in your financial life and not sure which way to go. If we've achieved this, the £9.95 that this book costs will have been very much worth the money!

APPENDIX I
EXAMPLE BUSINESS PLAN

I - Boozers Brewery Limited – The Concept

It's never been a better time to set up a new microbrewery. Drinkers in the UK are tired of the ubiquitous products of the big breweries like Greene King and Sharps and there's never been greater interest in the novel, the individual, and even the quirky amongst new beers.

There's no excepted definition of a microbrewery, but in this case we're talking about an output of two thousand gallons a week of three carefully crafted beers: a pale ale, a strong and "fruity" bitter, and a stout. The experience of hundreds of other microbreweries up and down the country has shown that a viable business can be run from small premises and using comparatively small initial resources, because of the tremendous thirst which exists amongst the drinking public for interesting and unusual beers.

But Boozers Brewery Limited is by no means just another microbrewery. There are two things which mark it out from the common herd. Firstly, the head brewer, Geoff Boozer, is not some enthusiastic amateur but a highly experienced professional, with 25 years' experience as head brewer in a substantial commercial brewery. Secondly, his unique formulation of a special kind of anti-freeze additive makes the beer, whilst qualifying as "real ale" in the eyes of the strictest CAMRA enthusiast, far longer lasting than conventional real ale, which will commend it to pub landlords tired of the chanciness and short life of real ales: as well as imparting a unique flavour to the beer. Geoff Boozer, from his long experience in the commercial sector, knows that the real key to success for a brewery is not getting drinkers to buy your beer, but getting publicans to buy your beer.

II – The Market

The market for the company's products comprises to a small extent beer wholesalers, who will no doubt distribute the beer nationwide; but principally direct sales to pubs within an approximately 25 mile radius of the brewery. This "catchment area", whilst not an absolutely rigid criterion, is intended to enable cost effective delivery, and also an effective sales initiative by way of visiting the various pubs (see below).

Within this area, there are currently 150 active free houses and 250 tied houses which are required to serve a guest beer. We calculate that, on expected levels of consumption, the brewery will be able to sell its production at full capacity if as little as 7% of these outlets take up the company's product.

We have taken fully into account the fact that this market is already fully served by other breweries, but we anticipate that our product will supplant other beers in a significant number of cases, due to the factors already mentioned of being easier to keep for longer periods, and its unique flavour.

As a second phase to the development of the business, we intend in due course to invest in bottling plant, which will enable us to sell bottled beers not just to pubs but also to supermarkets and other retail outlets.

III – Promotion and Marketing

The company's marketing drive is a two-pronged one. In attracting publicans' attention to the existence of an interesting new beer, there is no substitute for travelling around the whole catchment area, and talking to the various landlords. Allowance has been made for "free samples" of the beer to be provided to landlords as an incentive to stock the beer. If their customers then express approbation, they are likely to reorder. This sales work will be principally undertaken by the other director of the business, Geoff Boozer's brother Steve Boozer: who also has significant experience in the licensed trade.

The other prong of the company's proposed marketing attack is by means of social media, in particular Facebook, whose advertising is considered to be highly effective and comes at a comparatively low cost, sufficient to be included within the "other overheads" figure in the cash flow and the profit projections attached. The company's principal focus in marketing, however, is the direct approach to landlords mentioned first, with the social media advertising having a secondary role of promoting brand recognition when drinkers go into pubs in which the beers are available.

IV – The Competition

We have already commented that the pubs within the catchment area are currently, of course, already fully supplied with beer to their capacity. The competition of this company will come largely from other small and microbreweries in the area, since we will not be seeking to displace major national staples such as Greene King IPA and Doom Bar. We have considered in detail the other local breweries whose beers we confidently expect to displace, at least to some extent, and the principal ones are the following:

1. **The Grungetown Brewery**. The staple product of this brewery, Old and Twisted Bitter, is to be found in 21 pubs within the catchment area. Landlords have complained both about the short shelf life of the beer and the unreliability of deliveries: both areas in which we would plan to present publicans with a significantly better experience.

2. **Alice's Big Jugs Brewery**. Beer from this brewery, situated some 15 miles to the north east, is to be found in eight pubs within our chosen catchment area. Whilst this is a highly attractive product to the average beer consumer, publicans did complain that the beer is expensive, and the brewery is somewhat capricious and difficult to deal with. Our beers will typically sell at between £20 and £25 per barrel less than Alice's. We consider that this significant discount is made possible by the very low overhead base which is planned for Boozers Brewery, in contrast to the substantial pair of industrial units occupied by Alice's.

3. **Timid Tim's Ales.** At the other extreme, this brewery has very small premises and only half the number of fermenting vessels that form part of our plan. The brewery appears to be at full capacity, and we understand from landlords has difficulty fulfilling its promises. This is partly due to the fact that the single individual running the business has to deal both with the brewing process and all of the management and administrative part of the business, which we consider is not sustainable. Our business plan allows for the wages of two individuals, being Geoff Boozer full time on brewing and certain aspects of management, and Steve Boozer part time on sales and administrative functions.

4. **Deadman's Brewery**. This brewery has recently ceased production, and is only mentioned here as evidence of our research into the opportunities and difficulties faced by businesses of a similar scale in the same area. Deadman's Brewery made a very good start approximately three years ago, however due to the illness of the principal manager/sales operative with cirrhosis of the liver, it is now unable to continue to function. A clear distinction between business and leisure is very important in this industry.

V – The Investment Required

We are inviting a loan or loans totalling £100,000, which will be principally laid out in acquiring the necessary equipment and providing the company with working capital. (See the profit and loss and cash flow projections which form part of this document.) Security would be given over the equipment itself, and by way of floating charge over the company's stock, debtors and other fungible assets. The loan would commence repayment after a 5 year period given the anticipated profitability of the business, and would bear a 6% interest rate, within interest being paid quarterly. In addition, the lender(s) would be given discounted supplies of the company's product.

If potential investors wish to discuss these proposed terms, or substitute other forms of investment, we are open to discuss these: however, a comparatively short term and comparatively high interest bearing loan is our preferred option.

It would be noted that the cash flow forecast shows a negative balance on occasions throughout the year, after the payment of VAT and duty has been made. Negotiations for an appropriate level of overdraft are at an advanced stage with the bank. It is hoped that there is certain flexibility in the overdraft limit to allow for negative variances in the cash flow over that period: however the general approach in setting these projections has been a very prudent one.

VI – Profit and Loss and Cash flow Projections

These are to be found at the end of the plan, as appendices. The following are the key assumptions we have made in projecting these figures:

1. Sales will become substantial one month after production has commenced in April of the first year, with publicans typically paying for the beer two months after it has been supplied. Initially the brewery is expected to operate at something like one quarter of its total capacity, with this increasing during the first year to 62.5% capacity, or nearly full capacity at Christmas.

2. We have a firm quotation for the brewing equipment, which is included as a cash outflow in the first period.

3. Ingredients will be paid for on a 30 day credit period, and the anticipated gross profit percentage is derived from Geoff Boozer's experience of commercial brewing.

4. The rental has already been agreed in principle with the owner of the workshop from which the brewery will operate.

5. Other overheads include telephone, computer consumables (the equipment being provided by Geoff Boozer from his home), advertising, and small cash expenses.

6. VAT and duty will fall due quarterly, with the first payment being due in July.

7. The company's sales will grow gradually over a 5 year period to approximately 80% of capacity by the end of year five.

8. Other costs will increase, not necessarily reliably, but to some extent, with the greater capacity. After the end of the second year, a new employee will be taken on to undertake a wide range of administrative and production related duties; also Geoff and Steve Boozer will receive pay rises (subject to the success of the business being as anticipated) commensurate with the actual market value of their services.

9. The brewing equipment has a very long anticipated lifespan, and is indeed already second hand on acquisition. Therefore it is not felt necessary to provide for significant deprecation within the profit and loss account projection.

10. No capital repayments of the loan will be made within the first 5 years. However profits as shown will be retained and should be sufficient, on the basis of the projections, to repay the capital at the end of that period if the investors so require.

VII – Contingency Plans

The projections discussed above, and included as appendices to this document, are worked out on a highly prudent basis and it is anticipated that both cash flow and profitability will represent a significant improvement on the projections. However, the following contingencies have been considered in our planning.

1. Lower sales take-up. In the event that sales do not pick up as quickly as anticipated, there will, of course, be corresponding reductions in cash

outflows due to the purchase of ingredients and VAT and duty payments. Nevertheless, in the first year it is possible that company's overdraft facilities could be stretched in the event of sales being very markedly less than projected. In this event, as a temporary measure, Geoff Boozer will seek a personal loan to inject into the business. This is not sought as an initial part of the funding because of the expense involved in personal loan servicing.

2. Problems could arise with the equipment. For this reason a warranty is being sought for the first year, and problems arising after this time should hopefully be manageable within the company's anticipated cash flow, or indeed significantly lower cash flows.

3. All insurable contingencies will be included within the company's public liability and employer's liability insurance policies.

VIII – The People

Already introduced to some extent in the course of this business plan, the company will initially comprise a two man team, Geoff Boozer and his brother Steve Boozer.

Geoff has a degree in chemical engineering from Brunel University, and, after a period at United Breweries PLC in Burton-on-Trent, left to become the head brewer at Bobby's Beers in Nuneaton: he was the second youngest person ever to be appointed to a head brewer's post in a substantial commercial brewery in Great Britain. After 10 years at Bobby's Beers, he moved to become head brewer of the substantial brewery of Malebolge Chemical Industries at Burton-on-Trent.

Steve Boozer is a qualified chartered accountant who will deal with the financial aspects of the business in the intervals of his sales activities. As a chartered accountant, he is highly familiar with alcohol in all its forms, and brings to the business a highly developed network of pub landlords and managers.

Appendix A – Cash flow Forecast

BOOZERS BREWERY LIMITED
Cash Flow Forecast for the Year ended 31 March 2023

	April £'000	May £'000	June £'000	July £'000	August £'000	September £'000	October £'000	November £'000	December £'000	January £'000	February £'000	March £'000	Total £'000
Cash inflows													
Sales Income	0	0	0	10	15	20	25	25	35	25	25	25	205
Director's loans	10												10
External loans	100												100
	110	0	0	10	15	20	25	25	35	25	25	25	315
Cash outflows													
Brewing equipment	80												80
Professional set up costs	5												5
Purchases of ingredients		1	1	2	2	2	4	2	2	2	2	2	22
Wages	2	2	2	2	2	2	2	2	2	2	2	2	24
Heat light and power			5			5			7			6	23
Insurance	3												3
Rent	6			6			6			6			24
Other overheads	2	2	2	2	2	2	2	2	2	2	2	2	24
Loan Interest			1			2			1			2	6
VAT and duty				5			30			42			77
													0
	98	5	11	17	6	13	44	6	14	54	6	14	288
Opening bank balance	0	12	7	-4	-11	-2	5	-14	5	26	-3	16	
Net cash flow	12	-5	-11	-7	9	7	-19	19	21	-29	19	11	
Closing bank balance	12	7	-4	-11	-2	5	-14	5	26	-3	16	27	

Appendix B – Profit Projections

BOOZERS BREWERY LIMITED
Profit Projections for the Five Years ended 31 March 2027

	2023 £'000	2024 £'000	2025 £'000	2026 £'000	2027 £'000
Income					
Sales, net of VAT and duty	130	150	175	200	200
Expenditure					
Purchases of ingredients	13	15	18	20	20
Wages	24	24	48	48	48
Heat light and power	13	15	18	20	20
Insurance	3	3	4	4	5
Rent	24	24	24	24	24
Other overheads	24	24	30	30	30
Loan Interest	6	6	6	6	6
	107	111	147	152	153
Profit for the year before tax	23	39	28	48	47

Appendix C – Technical Information

The information contained in this appendix is confidential and is provided on the basis that the reader has agreed to sign an appropriate non-disclosure agreement. The recipes that will be used for the three beers are similar to those used by Geoff Boozer in his work for Malebolge Chemicals, however the unique aspect of the beers, which mark them out from other beers currently produced, is referred to as ingredient X. The main ingredient of this additive is ethylene glycol (CH2OH)2, however there is also a formulation of one part of nitric acid to two hundred parts of ethylene glycol and five parts of monosodium glutamate to the same number of parts of ethylene glycol.

This ingredient is produced inhouse from the raw materials which form part of the company's monthly purchases.

In tests, it has been shown that the addition of ingredient X to beer at a late stage of the fermenting process acts to extend its anticipated life by approximately 75%, in a series of controlled experiments. The addition of this also serves to mitigate the natural bitterness of the beer. One pint of ingredient X will typically be added to 100 gallons of beer at a late stage of fermentation, although these proportions will vary depending on the strength of the ultimate product.

APPENDIX II

VAT CATEGORIES

Outside the Scope

- Non business supplies.
- Supplier made outside the UK (but there may be a liability in the country of supply).
- Transfers of businesses as a going concern.

Exempt

- Sale or rent of land and buildings, except for new residential buildings, or commercial where there is an option to tax.
- Insurance and insurance booking.
- Postal services by a "universal service provider".
- Betting, gaming, and lotteries.
- Finance (investments, loans, and the services of intermediaries).
- Education in schools etc.
- Medical services and supplies by certain qualified practitioners.

- Undertakers.
- Subscriptions to trade unions and professional bodies.
- Sporting facilities.
- IHT exempt works of art.
- Fundraising events by charities.
- Cultural services by government and non-profit making bodies.
- Supplies where the supplier could not recover input tax.
- Investment gold
- Services by a group of exempt businesses to its members.

Zero-Rated

- Food (but not catering).
- Sewerage and water.
- Books, newspapers and magazines.
- Talking books etc for the blind.
- Sale and construction of new dwellings.
- Sale of dwellings created by conversion of non-residential buildings.
- Sale of "substantially reconstructed" listed buildings.
- Export of goods outside the EU and associated services.
- Passenger transport.
- Houseboats and (BS3632 complaint) and large caravans.
- Gold.
- Bank notes.
- Drugs, medicines and aids for the disabled.
- Charity shops, advertisements etc.
- Children's clothes.

- Supplies to ERIC (European Research Infrastructure Consortium).
- Women's Sanitary products.

Reduced Rates (5%)

- Domestic fuel or power.
- Installation of energy saving materials.
- Grant – funded installation of heating equipment or security goods, or connection of gas supply.
- Children's car seats.
- Conversions that change the number of dwellings in a building.
- Conversions to multiple occupancy dwellings.
- Conversions to residential homes, children's homes, and other residential institutions.
- Conversions of "empty homes".
- Contraceptives.
- Welfare advice by charities or public sector equivalents.
- Other large caravans.
- Cable cars.

Standard Rated (20%)

- All other supplies!

ALSO BY ALAN PINK FCA CTA

If you would like to learn more about tax planning for your business…

PRACTICAL TAX PLANNING FOR BUSINESS

Alan Pink FCA CTA
Paul Hyland FCA

HOW UK ENTREPRENEURS & INVESTORS CAN SAVE TAX LEGALLY & ETHICALLY

Available now on Amazon

Printed in Great Britain
by Amazon

20326105R00088